Persephone Book N° 80
Published by Persephone Books Ltd 2008

First published in 1934 by Country Life Ltd.

The publisher has made all possible efforts
to trace the owner of the copyright to the work
of Lucy H Yates

Endpapers taken from 'Spring', a 1933 rotary screen print on linen
by CPA Design printed by Calico Printers for Warner & Sons
© Warner Textile Archive
(Braintree District Museum Trust Ltd)

Prelim pages typeset in ITC Baskerville by
Keystroke, High Street, Tettenhall, Wolverhampton

Printed and bound in Germany by
GGP Media GmbH, Poessneck

978 1903155 707

Persephone Books Ltd
59 Lamb's Conduit Street
London WC1N 3NB
020 7242 9292

www.persephonebooks.co.uk

THE COUNTRY HOUSEWIFE'S BOOK:
HOW TO MAKE THE MOST
OF COUNTRY PRODUCE AND
COUNTRY FARE

THE COUNTRY HOUSEWIFE'S BOOK:
HOW TO MAKE THE MOST
OF COUNTRY PRODUCE AND
COUNTRY FARE

by

LUCY H YATES

✳✳✳✳✳✳✳

with decorations by

MARY GARDINER

PERSEPHONE BOOKS
LONDON

The Plan of the Book

PAGE

INTRODUCTORY NOTE   11

I   A GENERAL SURVEY OF STOREROOM AND
     LARDER   17

First preparations to make and what to
provide : Bottling Apparatus : The Spice-
Cupboard : A look round Larder and Cellar :
Methods of Producing a Low Temperature :
The Water-cooled Safe : Artificial Freezers:
Country Cooking Helps : The Fuelless
Cooker: The Pressure Cooker.

II   GARDEN AND ORCHARD FRUITS   27

How to Preserve by the Bottling Method :
How to Preserve as Jam and Jelly : Selected
Recipes for Jams, and Jellies : Marmalades :
Using Dried Fruits : Brandied Fruits
for Dessert : Fruit Juices, Cordials, etc.
Home-made Fruit Wines and other
Beverages.
Making Fruit Pulp. Storage of Fruit.
Preserving Fruit and Vegetables by Dry-
ing or Evaporation.

III   GARDEN VEGETABLE PRODUCE   89

Uncommon but profitable Vegetables to
grow : How to Keep Vegetables by Bottling,
by Pickling, etc. To make Chutney and

Ketchup, suggestions for Conserves : Use
of Mint : Uncommon Recipes for combining Vegetables with Cheese, etc., also use of
Rice, Lentils and Macaroni.

IV MILK AND EGGS   119

How to Deal with a Glut : Clotted Cream :
Cream Cheese-making, etc.: How to make
Butter, and what to avoid in making it :
Junkets : Curds and Whey : Uses of Curd :
Uses of Buttermilk : Skimmed Milk for
Toilet use, etc.

Eggs to Preserve : Important Points to
note : Brown Pickled Eggs : Egg and
Lemon Curd : Egg Emulsion : Egg Nogg :
Egg Wine.

V THE SPORTSMAN'S BAG   135

How to treat Game : To hang, pluck and
truss it: Cooking different kinds of game:The
grill and plank : Making Game Pies : Potted
Game: Jugged Hare: Wildfowl and the right
accompaniments to serve with each kind : To
make a Salmi of game-birds : Use of the
Casserole and Terrine : Potted Meats :
Venison : Venison Pasty : Venison Pudding : Rabbit Pie, Pigeon Pie, etc. Accessories to serve with game, etc.: Game Soups.

Freshwater fish : Trout, Salmon, Perch,
Pike and Carp, etc., Packing for transport :
Planking fish : Potted fish, Soused fish, etc.

The Plan of the Book

PAGE

VI   HERBS OF GRACE   157

Herbs for the Garden : Kitchen Herbs :
Wild Herbs : Pot-herbs to Pick and Store:
How to Dry and Keep : Dried Lavender and
Oil of Lavender : Flavouring Herbs :
Uses for Flowers and Leaves after Drying :
Pot Pourri.

Medicinal Herbs : The Common Camomile : Other Herbs and leaves for Teas :
Hops and their Drying, etc.

Fir Cones : Beech and Oak Leaves to
Keep: Leaf-Mould: Thistles and Bulrushes :
Packing Flowers and Leaves for the Post :
Drying Rose-Petals : A few suggestions
about Arrangement of Flowers.

VII HOBBIES OF THE COUNTRY HOUSEWIFE :
     AND SOME HOUSEHOLD PESTS AND
     FRIENDS   175

Keeping Bees : Rabbits, etc.: Treatment
of and Uses for Rabbit Skins : Using Fowl
and other Feathers.

Insect Pests and small Enemies : Moths,
Beetles and Cockroaches : Gnats and Aphis :
The Common House-fly : Wasps and Ants :
The Mischievous Mouse : Mites and
Spiders : Snails and Slugs : Pests injurious
to plants, bushes and trees : Scale, etc.

Unpaid Helpers of the Country Housewife.

PAGE

VIII   SPECIAL COUNTRY-HOUSE RECIPES   199

Household Bread and Norfolk Dump-
lings : Barm Cake : Lardy Cake : Tea-
Scones : Milk Batter Cakes : Raised Pies :
Meat Pies : Pig's Fry, etc. : Pickled Pork :
Sucking-pig : Sausages : Brawn : Curing
Bacon and Ham : Burnt Cream.

INTRODUCTORY NOTE

Introductory Note

THIS Book for the Country Housewife has been compiled with a view to making it complete without being confusing, full of suggestion and perhaps of inspiration, yet definite and practical. It is for the busy woman who must often look after the growing as well as the gathering of the crops, and who sometimes wants help in finding out what should be done with them at the right time.

It has been designed to aid people who are dependent upon their own resourcefulness and initiative, for in the country there is great need of these qualities. So often it is the unexpected that happens. There may, for instance, occur a glut of Milk, and it must be used to some good purpose or have to go down the drain ; or a crop of fruit or vegetable may reach the stage when it must be gathered or it will utterly spoil, yet the materials for preserving are not ready ; or some well-meaning friend drops a bag of game or half a dozen rabbits at the door, and everything else must be put aside in order to skin, pluck and use these at once. All these things may happen at any time to anyone who lives in the heart of the country away from shops and stores and where help is not to be had, and there is also that other emergency that all people with Country Houses, large or small, must be prepared to meet, namely, the arrival of unexpected guests at the time of a meal. This has become more frequent with the advent of the motor car. It is taken for granted that the Country-house larder is always stocked, that its storeroom is always full of home-made delicacies, and that there is always something ready to set upon the table. Of course it ought to be so, and the capable Country Housewife likes to believe that it is so, but she is not always able to live up to her standard. She is fallible, and it is so easy to forget to make certain things at the right time and to miss opportunities—and so hard to make up for such omissions !

Quite apart from necessary and practical things, if she is a true lover of the countryside, the Housewife likes to be able to collect from hedge and field, and make use of herbs and roots, leaves and flowers, and know to what purposes she can put these ; likewise the skins and feathers and other things that accumulate about her. Space has been given here to suggestions that will help in these matters, also to what can be done with other and far less welcome additions that intrude on her time and attention whether she will or no—to those household pests that trouble her wherever there is food in store, or fruit in course of ripening.

One especial difficulty which country folk have to meet we have tried to keep very prominent when compiling these pages, and that is the need for dealing with small pickings and tiny amounts, the " bits and bobs " that come in before a main crop is ready, and have either to be used or wasted. This is the particular problem of those who possess allotments or go down to a country cottage at week-ends, and suggestions are given for temporary methods of preservation that will answer the purpose until there is opportunity to carry out the usual process. For the sake of easy reference all the Recipes that belong to one kind of produce have been kept together in the section that deals, say, with Fruit, or with Vegetables, and so on. Anything to do with Fruit Preserving, whether Bottling, or making Jam, Jelly, Wines or Cordials, will be found in Section II, as well as the making of Fruit Pulp for temporary preservation, or storing fruit for long keeping. All Recipes that deal with green and root Vegetables, their cooking and serving as well as their preservation come into Section III ; Recipes for keeping and serving Game come into the section devoted to the Sportsman's Bag ; uses for Milk and the making of Butter, Clotted Cream and Cheese come together ; while Herbs, their collecting and drying, and suggestions for treating skins and feathers, are found in their own section. After these matters have been considered with all due seriousness and care, there have been added a number of standard and perhaps old-fashioned Recipes that a new generation of Country Housewives may be glad to have brought to their remembrance.

Even so, much has probably been omitted that ought to have found a place in these pages, and for that omission the only excuse is limitation of time and space. If, however, the housewife will add her own Recipes to those given here the book will become all the more her friend and helper, and if, in course of time, her copy of it comes to have a spot of grease and stain of brown earth on every other page, that will be taken as the greatest compliment that could be paid to its compiler.

L.H.Y.

A GENERAL SURVEY OF STOREROOM AND LARDER

1. *A General Survey of Storeroom and Larder*

IF the best use is to be made of pickings and small amounts, as well as of larger gatherings, it is essential to have in hand materials for preserving; bottles and jars in which to store what is preserved; with all the etceteras that belong to the work. If a supply of sugar, for instance, has to be ordered in a hurry it may not arrive in time ; if bottles and jars have to be sought out and cleaned at the time they are wanted that will cause annoyance : if rubbers are found to have perished and metal rings have rusted and the discovery is only made when bottling is actually being done, a good deal of useful material may go to waste. Therefore :

BEGIN EARLY in the season to make preparations by looking over the stock of bottles and jars, seeing that the steriliser and boiling-pan are ready for use, that the thermometer, the caps and rings, jam-pot covers, spoons, and all the other details are there in sufficient supply, that everything is clean and free of dust and placed just where it will be wanted.

To do all this well in advance saves much trouble and fatigue later ; also it quickens interest and stimulates the imagination, qualities that are very important where this kind of work is concerned, for without them it would be tedious and results might be—well, less than the best !

In a country town of any size one will usually find the Kilner Jar or the Fowler Lee bottling outfit is procurable, and the housekeeper who has not had experience of her own will be well advised to ask to have the method of using either type explained to her, even when she is confident that she knows all about them. There is very little to choose between these two most reliable types of bottle, the first-named, the Kilner, having a screw-on metal band, the second, the Fowler Lee, has the clip-on cap. Both require rubber rings to be inserted between the glass top and the bottle, and the purchaser should make sure that the glass is clear and smooth.

A sterilising pan is desirable because it is fitted with a rack for holding the bottles and has a double bottom, but if the housewife has a very large and deep fish-kettle she can quite well make this serve her purpose by herself making a false bottom with slats of wood tacked together, or using a thick layer of hay. As long as the cover fits well and the steam is kept in any pan that holds the bottles will do.

Always buy more rubber rings than will actually be needed, lest some have to be discarded, but the right number of screws will suffice. Where a good crop of fruit is anticipated some three or four dozen bottles will be wanted, and several dozen jars for jams and pickles. Buy prepared jam-pot covers in packets and corks for pickle-bottles, also sealing-wax for the latter.

When storing before use keep bottles and jars ranged in tiers upside-down to save getting dusty, and stand the steriliser on a wooden rack. Large wooden spoons cut on the slant are best for stirring jam.

THE SPICE-CUPBOARD

A most handy device is a diminutive chest of drawers each of which is labelled, or failing this a number of small tins kept on a set of shelves or in a bracket cupboard is a good method of storing spices, peppers, and the like. Sugar in quantities is kept in a lined case or wooden box ; the roughly-broken preserving sugar is usually sent out in such cases if bought by the half-hundredweight at a time. Vinegar is bought by the small cask.

The following list of Condiments with the amounts it will be advisable to have in stock, give some idea of what the Storeroom should hold where a fair supply of preserves and pickles, etc., is likely to be made :

Whole and Ground Peppers	$\frac{1}{4}$-lb. each.
Common Salt	$\frac{1}{2}$ stone.
Brown Sugar	$\frac{1}{2}$ stone.
Preserving Sugar	1 cwt.
Whole and Ground Ginger	$\frac{1}{2}$-lb. each.
Mace and Cinnamon (stick)	2-ozs. ,,
Cloves and Nutmegs	2-ozs. ,,
Cayenne Pepper	$\frac{1}{2}$-oz.
Allspice	2-ozs.
Mustard Seed	2-ozs.

Sultana raisins and Chillies will be needed where Chutney is being made, but can be bought when required.

The Store-cupboard should also hold supplies of the following requisites, kept in their separate boxes :

Sealing-wax ;	Paraffin Wax ;
Gummed labels ;	Parchment paper ;
Jam-pot covers, waxed	Corks ;
rounds, etc. ;	Fine String.

A Look round Larder and Cellar

Bottling and Preserving do not cover all requirements in the way of storing and saving even in the quite small Country House ; Salting, Pickling, Curing and Drying have all to be considered, and very often all these methods have to be used. Now that preservatives are not permitted in trade articles housewives are encouraged to cure and pickle their own bacon and meats, even when they cannot smoke-dry them. Experienced housekeepers keep in hand a tub of Brine Pickle, finding that a most useful resource, while others use a Marinade for fish and fowl, finding this an excellent method for anything that has to be kept only a few days. A Marinade, by the way, is made of equal parts of Vinegar, Wine and Water (a cheap white wine is best), and is flavoured with an onion stuck with cloves, with bay-leaves, slices of lemon, whole peppers and a little salt. The mixture is boiled afresh each day and poured over meat, birds or fish when cold, these remaining in it for 3 to 5 days.

Brine

To make a small tub of Brine it is usual to allow three or four times as much water as is required to dissolve, say, a couple of pounds of rock salt. Some brown sugar and a bag of spices and peppers are added, while a little salt-petre dissolved in it improves the colour of meats. Pickling Brine is used for beef, mutton, pork and tongues, the method of Dry-salting being preferred for bacon and ham.

Methods of Producing a Low Temperature

To keep cellars and store-places cool is often difficult in summer weather where country cottages have no special provision for good ventilation without dust and flies. In newly-constructed cottages and bungalows the larder is often inadequate and the ventilation poor and there are no stone benches on which to stand food as in the older house that is supplied with underground cellarage. In modern houses it is taken for granted that people will have refrigerators and ice-chests and portable safes—as is also taken for granted that their owners will have the money to buy these somewhat expensive luxuries !

THE WATER-COOLED SAFE

Happily there is a quite inexpensive device for producing coolness by evaporation, that will answer the housewife's purpose very well as long as it is kept supplied with moisture. In principle it is the same as the old-fashioned butter-cooler that consisted of an overturned flower-pot set in a dish of water.

The safe itself can be the quite ordinary one consisting of light wooden frame and sides of perforated zinc. On the top of this stands a bowl or deep tray filled with water, and depending from this strips of cheesecloth hang over the safe. As long as there is water in the tray and the strips are wet the temperature within the safe will be several degrees cooler than that outside it.

The zinc or clay butter-cooler standing in a deep dish containing water, a wet cloth over it, is a resource of nearly every country housewife, and there are few better methods of keeping small quantities of butter or cream cool in the hottest weather, while a jar of porous clay standing in a bowl of water will keep milk or anything inside it cool and sweet. The principle of air passing over a moist surface can be applied in various ways to the keeping of food, both fresh and cooked, as long as water does not come in actual contact with the foods.

ARTIFICIAL ICE-MAKING FREEZERS

There is much to be said in favour of the mechanical ice-making freezer for a country house or cottage in districts where cream is plentiful, since by its help the most delightful desserts can be made with little trouble. It is well to be warned, however, that in very hot weather this may not work as satisfactorily as it does in cold because the chemicals alter in character. The freezing-mixture is composed of ammonium nitrate and common washing soda ; if equal quantities of each are dissolved in the same amount of water the temperature is reduced by as much as 55 degrees and ices will become quite firm even when made of rich cream. Many delightful desserts and puddings can be produced by the help of the artificial ice-making machine of small dimensions, making it an investment worth having.

COUNTRY COOKING HELPS : THE FUELLESS COOKER

A very real help to a country housekeeper is to have a Fuelless Cooker.

This may be a homely Hay-box or something rather more elaborate made on the same principle. Many people who have not used such a cooker are sceptical of its ability to save time and trouble, but a little experiment with it soon convinces them of their error and with understanding comes conviction.

The hay-box is a development of the idea of the Thermos Flask in that where air cannot enter and where there is no contact with the atmosphere heat once gained is retained for a very long time. When food is brought to boiling-point and placed in the hay-box it retains that heat for hours, just as hot liquids in the Thermos remain hot for a long time. In the Cooker this heat is maintained by hot-iron discs placed in metal frames that are at the bottom of the box, so that not only is heat maintained, but cooking actually proceeds, thus the Fuelless Cooker is something more than a mere heat-retainer.

To make one a stout wooden case with well-fitting lid on hinges is necessary ; this is lined with felt, two layers being better than one, then with folds of news-paper, the lid being similarly padded. The stewpans or jars containing food stand above the heated discs, themselves being at boiling heat, and are padded round with folds of paper. The lid is clamped down and the box left to its own devices. Porridge placed in overnight is hot and fully-cooked in the morning ; stew put there in the morning is hot and not overcooked by evening. Thus time and attention are saved as well as any occasion for watching and stoking the fire.

The Pressure Cooker

This touches the other extreme by expediting the time required for the process, although it does not lessen the need for giving the usual time to preparation. As a Pressure Cooker can be used over an oil flame just as well as over a gas jet it is certainly a useful help in a country kitchen, for it produces a roast, cooks vege-tables and a pudding all at the same time, and in the most expeditious manner, after they have been trimmed, mixed, and put together. A preliminary browning in hot fat is necessary to give a fowl a pleasing appear-ance or to make a roast of meat look appetising ;

otherwise the cooking is perfectly done and the flavour of everything remains true, no one thing affecting another. The time required is set by the whistle, which gives warning that cooking is done, when heat should be turned off, and when the pressure is relaxed the cover can be removed. For saving time and ensuring success the Pressure Cooker is admirable, but neither it nor the hay-box will boil water ! For a kettle and a boiling-pan the country housewife must still use either a fire or an oil-stove when neither gas nor electricity are available.

GARDEN AND ORCHARD
FRUITS

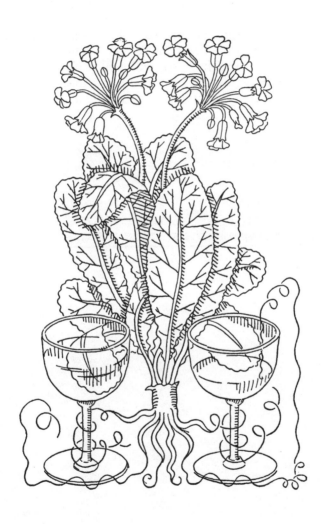

II

1. *How to Preserve by the Bottling Method*

EING provided with such tools and materials as she is likely to need the country housewife can give her attention to watching the growth of her crops, and to studying such means as she may take to improve the yield. Some country people, for instance, make it a practice to thin-out growing fruit, especially gooseberries, while still small, as this allows the berries to grow to a more even size. Fruit removed by thinning is not wasted but finds some use in the kitchen. In going over currant bushes, too, they turn down top shoots, not breaking them off but leaving them to wither away, as in this way the sap is turned back to swell the fruit instead of being wasted in making useless leafage. It is possible, too, to take early steps to stop the ravages of grubs and flies and to apply an insecticide in early stages but not in later ones.

PICKING FRUIT

A busy housewife who finds it inconvenient to give the time to bottling or otherwise preserving large quantities, is very glad to be able to pick small amounts, and to deal with these at convenient moments without interfering with other household duties and by processes that cannot always be adopted where a bigger crop has to be treated.

THE TIME TO PICK

The best time for picking fruit is in the evening at the close of a dry day, and it saves trouble if the first rough sorting is done then. The best fruit of the most even size should be saved for bottling while the mixed sizes will do very well for boiling as jam. One advantage of sorting whilst picking is that if the yield proves insufficient for preserving by one method plans can be altered and some other measure adopted. Then, too, such preliminary processes as "topping and tailing" can also be done in the evening and so save time and trouble afterwards.

FRUIT FOR BOTTLING

When picking with a view to filling bottles it is better to use fruit as even in size as may be for although small fruit may seem useful in filling up spaces, it has a tendency to go to a mash and cloud the appearance. Large fruit is certainly wasteful of space, therefore that of medium size is most suitable for filling bottles and preserving by that method. It matters little about mixing large and small together when making Jam, and when intending to make Jelly it is unnecessary to "top and tail" berries or strip currants, providing they are perfectly clean, as for that purpose all fruit is strained through a bag. For Bottling, however, it is necessary to sort carefully, pick over, and grade the size of all fruit.

PACKING FRUIT IN BOTTLES

When packing into bottles use two strips of wood, flattened at the ends, with which to coax the fruit into place, and shake the bottles vigorously when filling them to ensure getting as much fruit as possible into the space, indeed with hard fruits like gooseberries, cherries and plums some pressure may be used. After a bottle is packed fill up with water or with syrup until it runs over the top, then put on the rubber ring, passing the finger round to see that this lies perfectly flat, press down the glass cap, put on the clip or metal screw, and make this *nearly* tight. The screws are not screwed down tightly until after sterilisation. The bottles are now ready to place in the sterilising pan, and should rest on a false bottom as before-mentioned, but should not touch each other.

Bottling Green Gooseberries, Cherries and Plums

For common use green gooseberries are bottled with water only, but a better colour and flavour is ensured by using a light syrup ; this applies also to cherries and plums. A light syrup does not altogether do away with the need of adding sugar later, but it brightens the colour and improves the appearance and to some extent improves the flavour.

Light and Heavy Syrups

Syrup is " light " or " heavy " according to the quantity of sugar used.

Half a pound of sugar to a pint of water makes a light syrup ; three-quarters of a pound to a pint makes a heavy one.

Method of Making Syrup

Dissolve the sugar in half the water and boil until clear, then add the remainder of water cold, and use the syrup when quite cold.

Bottling Soft and Juicy Fruits

Fruits like ripe currants and raspberries, which exude a deal of juice do not need either syrup or water to be added to them, but are nicest if when filling the bottles some soft sugar is sprinkled over the fruit *dry*. Shake vigorously to get as much fruit as possible into the bottle. When sterilised these bottles will be full of rich syrup and the fruit will be bright in colour.

How to Sterilise

The pan is filled with cold water, sufficient to come over the top of the bottles if deep enough, but at any rate enough to cover the shoulder, for when using a fish-kettle it is generally not possible to do more than this, but the deep lid that collects the steam inside it makes up any deficiency of depth.

Set the filled pan over a low gas, small fire or oil-stove, and let it quite slowly reach the temperature given in each recipe, after which, in order to keep at that temperature it may be necessary to lower the heat. It must be remembered that sterilisation is done at considerably below boiling-point ; where bottles stand in boiling water the fruit is forced up to the top and the appearance of the packing is completely spoiled.

Taking Bottles out of the Pan

About this a word of caution may be necessary. It sounds easy to say " Lift the bottle and test the seal," but is not easy to do when the pan is full of scalding water. The best plan is to bale out some water and then lift each bottle by the cap, using a soft cloth for handling, set on the table, and at once tighten the pressure of the screw or clip.

Never set hot bottles on cold stone or marble, and keep them out of draught.

Leave for twenty-four hours before testing to see if the seal is perfect. This seal, by the way, is the vacuum that is created at the top underneath the cap, that is to say, a space without air. This it is that keeps the contents sweet and holds the cap firmly in position. In order to know whether this vacuum has been created lift the bottle by the cap alone, having removed screw or clip, doing it cautiously at first, and if it holds, give a little shake to make sure it is tight ; then wipe the bottle dry and put it away on a shelf.

It is possible that the seal is *not* perfect, that the vacuum has *not* been created at the first time of sterilising, and if so the cap will easily come off when you attempt to raise it. When this happens, remove the cap, examine to see if there is any defect like a roughness in it, or an imperfection in the rubber ring ; change that for another one, set cap and ring back in place, re-sterilise the bottle, bringing it up to the same temperature exactly as before. The second time it is fairly sure to be all right.

When putting bottled fruits away on the shelf, preferably away from the light, wipe and polish well, remove metal rings or caps and put these away in a drawer for use again, and label bottles where necessary. Never put away with rings or clips remaining on them, as these will inevitably rust and be exceedingly difficult to remove when that bottle is wanted for use.

BOTTLING IN THE OVEN

This is a ready way of doing one or two bottles at a time when they are not wanted for long keeping, and providing the oven is hot it saves any trouble with water and a pan, and answers very well indeed for soft fruits such as currants, raspberries and blackberries.

Fill the bottles with fruit right up to the top, sprinkle liberally with dry soft sugar as filling proceeds, adding no water at all ; put on the caps, but no rubbers or rings.

Stand the bottles on the oven shelf but place thick paper or cardboard between shelf and bottle. Close the oven and gradually increase the heat but do not let it reach baking heat. Watch the bottles and when the fruit seems to have sunk down to about three-quarters of the original amount, take them out and quickly fill up by using the contents of one bottle to add to the rest. Then put on wet rubbers, and caps and screw down tightly. If done quickly a vacuum will form of its own accord. Many people, however, tie paper or a piece of bladder-skin over the top, to further ensure keeping ; as a rule fruit that is bottled in the oven is intended for ready consumption and is not expected to keep very long.

TOMATOES

Tomatoes for quick consumption may be bottled in the oven precisely like other fruit, using a little salt in place of sugar and tying down with bladder-skin after putting on the cap. This, of course, is a quick and ready means of conserving them for kitchen use.

If required for other purposes, such as for salads in the winter-time, it is worth while to bottle fine tomatoes after the same manner as other fruit, using salt instead of sugar, and water to fill up the bottle. *Sterilise for half an hour at* 190 *degrees* after allowing an hour to reach this temperature.

Small fruit packs more easily than large, and tomatoes, especially, should be under-ripe ; it is well also to skin them before packing by steeping in scalding water a minute or two, after which the skins can easily be drawn off. They can also be halved or quartered, and so will pack many more into the same space.

Blanching Pears and Apples

Before bottling pears and apples it is an improvement to their appearance to blanch them, as otherwise they are apt to go a little rusty. This is sometimes done by the sulphur method, described below, sometimes by merely throwing the fruit as it is peeled and quartered into water containing lemon-juice.

Sulphuring Jars For Blanching Purposes

A word as to this may be inserted here as, although little practised now, it is a method that is useful where damp is to be feared, and it is also a good method of blanching fruits before they are bottled if they lose colour easily.

The easiest way to proceed is to set light to some dry powdered sulphur held in an old iron spoon, and to insert this under an overturned glass jar. As soon as one jar is full of sulphur-smoke slip out the spoon and put it under another one, and so on until a number have been filled with the smoke. If the fumes die down use fresh sulphur and light up again.

When blanching portions of fruit drop these into the jar containing sulphur fumes and cover the top, leaving the fruit several minutes. No flavour will be imparted, but the whiteness will be kept until a number of portions are ready for bottling or other uses.

Housewives of a former generation invariably sulphured all their jars before putting-up their preserves, trusting to this to keep them from going mouldy or from fermenting. A later generation has found other and readier methods more satisfactory, but the old one still has value when blanching is needed.

For easy reference we will now take fruits in the

order of their ripening and give brief directions for
bottling each kind.

EARLY RHUBARB

Use while small and young and of bright red colour.
Measure the length of the bottle or jar and cut to same,
fill by inserting stalks upright, wedging them tightly ;
add water or syrup (cold), put on rubbers and caps,
screw down and sterilise by bringing temperature up
to 130 degrees within an hour, raise to 165 *degrees and
keep at this for* 20 *minutes,* then remove from pan and
screw down tightly. This is very pleasing in appearance and makes a nice dessert when syrup has been
used.

GOOSEBERRIES and CURRANTS have been described,
but :

RASPBERRIES

deserve special mention because if the fruit is very
large and fine it pays to take the trouble to fill the
hollow that is left after taking out the stalk with a ripe
red currant, taking care this stays in place when packing
the bottle. Use a heavy syrup for raspberries as this
is truly a dessert fruit. Bring the temperature up to
165 *degrees in the first hour* and *keep at that for* 15
minutes.

STRAWBERRIES

These are not a good bottling fruit, being far nicer
as jam, but a few varieties give fairly satisfactory results, among them " Sir Joseph Paxton " and " Royal
Sovereign ". The berries should be uniform in size,
neither large nor small, as nearly perfect as possible.
A heavy syrup should be used with them as this is

purely a dessert fruit. In order to ensure a good result it is better to make the syrup with the juice of currants instead of water, and then a better flavour will be obtained as well as a better colour. After packing the bottles and filling full with this rich syrup, then putting on the rubber rings, caps and screw bands or clips, *sterilise at* 160 *degrees for half an hour.*

CHERRIES

The best cherries for bottling are the red and acid varieties such as the Morella and May Duke. Morellas are very satisfactory for all methods of preserving, i.e., as jam or as candied fruit as well as for bottling and for making a sweet pickle. There is much demand for red cherries canned, or in sweet syrup for the confectionery trade, and also as candied fruit for decorative purposes. White cherries when canned or bottled lack flavour and are apt to lose their pinky tinge, while black ones, unless very rich and fleshy, are apt to taste flat.

In bottling cherries pack closely and use heavy syrup for filling, then bring slowly to 190 *degrees and keep at that heat for* 10 *minutes.*

APRICOTS AND PEACHES

Cut in halves and remove stones, cracking a few of these for the kernels, which blanch and split in halves. Arrange the portions very neatly in bottle or jar, letting the halves overlap each other as closely and regularly as possible. Fill up to the brim with heavy syrup, add rings and caps and screw down tightly. Sterilise by bringing up to 190 *degrees, keeping at this temperature for* 10 *minutes.*

35

PLUMS (GREEN)

Green or Egg Plums that will be used for cooking may be bottled somewhat under-ripe by wedging as many as possible into the jars or other containers, using a thin syrup or even plain water for covering and sterilising at 165 *degrees for one hour.* Make sure the seal is sound.

GREENGAGE OR VICTORIA PLUMS

Choose firm and slightly under-ripe fruit and use heavy syrup for filling the bottles ; bring the temperature up to 165 *degrees* and then *reduce during the next half-hour,* when lift out to cool.

Large Victorias may be treated like apricots and cut in halves, removing the stones and laying the halves over each other hollow side downwards. They make a very good appearance this way.

DAMSONS

These bottle quite successfully, but are much better if preserved as jam after the stones have been removed by rubbing the fruit through a wire sieve.

APPLES AND PEARS

Bottling of these is, as before mentioned, a little difficult as they are apt to discolour quickly ; on this account keep a bowl of water at hand and throw in the halves of fruit immediately after peeling and coring. A little vinegar or lemon-juice in the water keeps the fruit white.

Fill bottles carefully, laying halves neatly over each other, or quarters together.

More fruit can be packed into a bottle if it is first softened by putting the fruit into a steamer for 3 or 4 minutes to scald and slightly cook the pieces, then they lie more closely and pack more easily. This is especially wise when dealing with pears, and a few drops of cinnamon essence added to the syrup used to fill up the bottle of pears, or of ginger to apples, is an improvement.

Time to sterilise : *Apples,* bring slowly up to 165 *degrees and keep at that for* 1½ *hours.* *Pears,* bring slowly to 190 *degrees and keep at that for 45 minutes,* in all about 1½ hours.

LOGANBERRIES

This berry is very apt to contain a white maggot, and it is advisable to soak in a weak salt solution for a couple of hours to draw out the maggot ; then rinse well in cold water and pack firmly, filling the bottles. Use rather unripe fruit, otherwise it will go to a mash. A heavy syrup is desirable.

Time to sterilise : *bring temperature to* 130, *raise to* 150, and keep at that *for* 15 *minutes,* taking in all 1½ hours.

2. *How to Preserve as Jam and Jelly*

MERELY to boil fruit and sugar together does not make Jam. It is rather necessary to state this somewhat emphatically, as there are people who never reason about things and content themselves with following an old custom, or some haphazard idea of their own and still expect results to turn out all right. Making jam, however, is a scientific process as well as a real test of skill. It requires some knowledge of the change that takes place in fruit itself at various stages of ripening, as well as some experience of the method of making. The " setting " and the flavour, the appearance and the keeping quality all depend on the presence in the fruit of a certain natural gelatinous substance called "Pectin", and upon it being there in sufficient amount. It is necessary, therefore, to be able to judge the stage when pectin is plentiful and pick the fruit at that time. Usually this is when the fruit is slightly under-ripe ; as fruits grow sweeter and more juicy the pectin diminishes. In some fruits, such as the strawberry and cherry, pectin is so deficient in amount that it is necessary to use the acid juice of gooseberries or currants with these fruits when making jam while to other sweet fruits like apricots and peaches we add lemon-juice or even tartaric acid. A rather popular product known as " Certo " is a pure fruit extract and can therefore be commended for use when making jam from fruit that has been left too long before it was picked.

Other points to note about the making of Jams, Jellies and Marmalades, are the need for boiling the fruit first, with enough water at the bottom of the pan to prevent catching, and the need for constant stirring at this stage until a soft pulp is obtained ; also not to add the sugar until the fruit has been thoroughly cooked. *It is the fruit that requires cooking and not the sugar.* On attention to this point depends the flavour, the bright colour, and the setting of the preserve. Over-boiling after the sugar has been added is the reason why the jam candies on the top, is treacly in texture and dark in colour. Boiling sugar so quickly passes from one stage to another, from a thin syrup to a thick one, and from that to a caramel, that all cooking of the fruit should be done before any sugar goes into the pan.

Another point is to prevent any check to the boiling such as takes place when sugar is added cold to boiling fruit. After weighing out the amount required according to the weight of fruit used the sugar should be spread out on trays or dishes and set in the oven to become quite hot. It may candy a little as it gets hot, but that is no detriment to it. When it is poured into the boiling fruit it makes a hissing sound, melts very quickly, and does not check the heat more than a very little. Times for boiling the jam or jelly *after* sugar has been added are given in each recipe.

MIXING FRUITS

Here are a few suggestions for combining fruits that will be especially useful to people who have only small quantities at a time to deal with :

Use the juice of Red Currants when making

Raspberry,
Strawberry, and
Cherry Jam.

(Or the juice from under-ripe Gooseberries.)

Use a little Rhubarb finely shred when making Black Currant Jam or Jelly.

Use the juice of Lemons, Limes or Grapefruit when making

> Marrow Jam,
> Apple Jam,
> Peach or Pear Marmalade,
> Tomato Preserves.

Blackberries also need the addition of some acid unless combining them with sour apples for jam or jelly.

FOUR-FRUIT JAM OR JELLY

Another suggestion for people who have very small quantities of mixed fruits to deal with is to combine them and use level quantities ; say of cherries, strawberries, raspberries and gooseberries ; to boil them together until very soft, crush and strain through coarse muslin, measure the juice obtained and boil that with three-quarters of its amount of white sugar ; boil rapidly for ten minutes, pour into glasses and let it set before covering. (Or use the fruits without straining if preferred.)

PREPARING FRUIT FOR JAM

Careful cleansing is another point to note.

It is well to rinse all stem fruit under the cold-water tap, but plums and other firm fruit should be wiped with a cloth. Gooseberries, except for making jelly, require topping and tailing ; currants, again, except when making jelly, require stripping from the stalk ; raspberries and loganberries require very careful picking over and inspecting for grubs. Strawberries require the hulls to be removed while bruised portions of apricots and peaches should be cut away. Rhubarb should be wiped with care and cut across in short lengths, or evenly shred, to avoid its becoming stringy. Marrows cook better if cut in short strips after peeling.

Seeds and peelings, pips and parings, by the way, yield much pectin ; they should be separately boiled and strained and the liquid added to the pan instead of plain water.

The Boiling Pan

A brass or copper preserving-pan, such as used to be so highly prized, is not regarded with much favour in these days when aluminium and enamelled iron are so much easier to keep clean, and are also less liable to burn. Whatever type of pan is used it must be scrupulously clean and smooth at the bottom, and should have a little water put in first, or be rubbed over with lard.

Weighing Fruit and Sugar

A " rough and ready " method is to weigh the pan first, then to weigh it again after the picked fruit has been put in. This can be done where there is only a Salter's balance to use, and in such case one would buy sugar in packets of specified weight and judge the proportions accordingly.

A more accurate method is to use scales and to weigh the fruit after its picking and cleansing and before it goes into the pan. One would weigh the sugar, too, before spreading it on dishes for heating.

Procedure

Make the pan hot and pour in a little water first ;

then put in the fruit, stirring frequently to keep it from catching, keep stirring at intervals all the time it is cooking until it is reduced to a pulp and seems to be evenly cooked. For stirring purposes use a large wooden spoon, preferably one that is cut across in a slant, as this pushes the pulp about better than a rounded one. Usually it takes about half an hour's gentle boiling to reduce fruit to the right stage before adding sugar to turn it into jam ; (when boiling for jelly it can be cooked a little longer with advantage.) For jam the sugar would then be put into the pan ; for jelly the fruit would be turned into a bag and strained.

RAPID BOILING

The more rapidly jam or jelly boils the shorter time will it need to remain over the fire ; during the time that it is boiling attention must not be relaxed and stirring must be constant. Rapid boiling for half an hour will cause less wastage than slow boiling for an hour which so many think to be necessary. With rapid boiling the colour is kept bright ; with slow boiling it is darkened.

FINISHING PROCESSES

Jars for holding the jam or jelly should be made as hot as they can be handled by warming them in the oven (after they have been washed and polished). They should be filled to the brim with the boiling preserve and can be covered at once if standing on a tray or table where they can remain until cool enough to handle. Use the circles of waxed paper and the covers that are to be bought in packets as these save much time and are neat in appearance.

Small half-pound jars are best for jelly, pound jars for finer jams, larger ones for marmalades and kitchen jams. If these cardinal points be remembered, i.e., that it is the fruit that requires cooking most ; that rapid boiling for a short time keeps the colour bright ; that jars should be heated and covering done quickly ; much of the labour of preserving will be shortened and the result will be satisfactory.

Straining of Fruit for Making Jelly

Beyond stating that fruit need not be stripped or picked from the stalk when it is intended for making jelly, nothing has been said as yet about that most important process of straining. Many people prefer to make jelly rather than jam from fruits such as currants in order to be saved the trouble of stripping.

There is all the same the extra trouble of straining pulp and liquor through a bag, and there is some loss of material to be expected, nevertheless the storeroom is not complete without we have some red currant jelly in reserve, some black currant also, and blackberry and apple, with other jellies such as quince and medlar if we can obtain them.

The Bag for Straining Fruit

The materials for the bag can be hessian, fine canvas, or very coarse calico. It should be a square piece folded to make a cone with pointed end and wide top, with loops of stout tape sewn to the top. It is best to suspend it between the legs of an upturned chair, when the basin can be put on the seat that is then upside down. Do not squeeze a jelly-bag if you want the liquor to be bright, but for " second-best " a little squeezing is allowable.

43

A pint of clear juice and a pound of fine sugar are the usual proportions for best quality jelly. Add a little lemon-juice to the liquor if the fruit is very sweet. This is especially desirable when using apples.

A Note of Warning

QUANTITIES

In the Recipes that follow the quantities given can be halved or further reduced by dividing them in the same proportion. The amounts here named would not be more than would be gathered from the average country garden at any single picking, but the small-holder need not be deterred from using a recipe by thinking she is under the necessity of keeping exactly to the quantities named. Provided she keeps to the same *proportions* she may reduce the amounts as much as she pleases, and similarly she may increase them if blessed with a very prolific garden or orchard !

TOTAL TIME NOT STATED

The total time required for making fruit into jam or jelly has not been stated in the following Recipes, but only that for boiling *after the sugar has been added.* The reason for this is that some fruits take longer to cook to a pulp, others quickly break up and become soft, and the jam-maker is the best judge, or will be after she has gained a little experience. Roughly speaking, however, half an hour's boiling is sufficient to cook the fruit thoroughly well. Very soft fruits make much juice and need less preliminary boiling than hard berries and stone fruit. When making marmalade, however, three-quarters of an hour's preliminary boiling is necessary, and longer may be an advantage.

SELECTED RECIPES FOR JAMS AND JELLIES

Apricot Jam

> 5-lbs. fresh fruit ;
> 5-lbs. lump sugar ;
> 1 pint of water.

Method

Wash the fruit, cut in quarters, remove stones. Put the fruit into the pan with the water and slowly bring to boil and cook slowly until soft and reduced. Crack open a few stones and split the kernels then add to the fruit. Stir frequently to prevent catching. Add the sugar and bring quickly to boiling-point ; boil for 15 minutes, stirring all the time, then remove from heat and pot down at once.

If using dried apricots soak in water to cover well for at least a night, and add only half a pint when boiling the fruit.

Apple and Blackberry Jam

> 4-lbs. blackberries (washed) ;
> 2-lbs. sliced apples (tart variety) ;
> 1 pint water ;
> 5-lbs. sugar.

Cook the blackberries first with the water and then rub them through a hair-sieve. Pare and slice the apples and cook these separately, then add the sieved blackberries, bring to the boil and cook five minutes ; add the hot sugar and continue boiling, stirring all the time, for 10 to 15 minutes, testing it for setting before removing from the fire.

BLACKBERRY JELLY

For Blackberry Jelly (which apple improves) pass both fruits through the jelly-bag after cooking until they have yielded all the juice they will, and allow an equal weight of sugar. If sour apples are used there will be no need to add more acid.

ANOTHER RECIPE FOR BLACKBERRY JELLY

5-lbs. blackberries, carefully picked over ;
1 pint of water ;
1-lb. sugar to each pint of juice ;
5 tablespoonfuls lemon-juice.

Boil the berries with the water and lemon-juice over low heat for about an hour, or longer if there seems to be more goodness to extract. Strain the juice through the jelly-bag, then weigh before returning to the pan. Bring up to boiling-point, add the heated sugar, and boil well for 10 or 15 minutes and test for setting. Put up in small jars.

BLACK CURRANT JAM

5-lbs. picked currants, 1-lb. rhubarb ;
3 pints of water ;
7-lbs. sugar.

Stem the currants and cut the rhubarb across in shreds. Boil with the water until the fruit is thoroughly soft. Stir constantly as it is apt to catch at the bottom. When fruit is a pulp, add the sugar and boil fast for 15 minutes but not more, stirring all the time. It should set very quickly.

CHERRY JAM

> 4-lbs. Morella or May Duke Cherries (weigh after removing stones) ;
> 3-lbs. sugar ;
> Juice of 2 large lemons, or ½ teaspoonful tartaric acid.

Stone the cherries and tie stones in muslin, putting this into the pan with the fruit and water. Add lemon-juice at same time. Boil gently or simmer, for about thirty minutes, lift out the stones and add the sugar, then boil briskly for ten minutes or rather longer.

Morella cherries are sour and slightly less acid will be necessary. With May Dukes a proportion of red currant juice can be used instead of adding other acid.

Put up Cherry Jam in small glasses.

CURRANT JELLY (RED)

> 8-lbs. Ripe Currants ;
> 4-lbs. granulated sugar.

It is not necessary to stem the currants first, but to wash well and dry in the sun ; boil gently with enough water to cover the bottom of the pan, and the pan can be covered while the fruit is reducing. Strain through a bag and weigh the juice ; return to pan, bring to the boil, add sugar made hot, and boil just ten minutes from time it has come to boiling-point.

Put up in small glasses.

Currant Jelly should be a brilliant colour, firm but not stiff, and sharp in flavour.

Black Currant Jelly is made in the same way, but rather more sugar is necessary.

DAMSON JAM

> 4-lbs. damsons ;
> 4-lbs. sugar ;
> 1½ pints water.

Wash the damsons and put them into the preserving-pan with the water and cook gently, stirring now and then, until the fruit is well broken down. Remove stones as they rise, but they will not readily come to the surface until the sugar is in and has boiled up. Boil, after adding the sugar, until a little shows signs of setting. Judgment is the best guide, while stirring and clearing of stones should be continuous.

GREEN GOOSEBERRY JAM

> 4-lbs. gooseberries ;
> Equal weight of sugar ;
> 1½ pints of water.

Top and tail the berries and boil with the water until well broken down and softened ; if taken when fully-grown and just before they change colour the jam will be a fine pinky red when finished ; a green jam is not to be commended.

Add the sugar hot, and boil for 10 to 15 minutes after the jam has come again to boiling-point. This should set firm quite quickly, and keep well.

GREENGAGE JAM

> 3-lbs. greengages ;
> 3-lbs. sugar ;
> 1 pint water.

Cut the fruit in half, removing the stones. Break

a few and add the kernels to the fruit. Put fruit in pan with the water and bring to the boil and keep gently cooking for 15 minutes. Add the sugar, boil up, boil rapidly, stirring well, and allow not more than ten minutes more. Test for setting.

MARROW JAM

> 1 large marrow, cut in pieces after paring and removing seeds ;
> To 4-lbs. of cut marrow add 3½-lbs. sugar ;
> 4-ozs. root ginger ;
> 2 lemons, juice and rind ;
> 2-ozs. preserved ginger.

Cut the marrow in small pieces after paring and removing the seeds and pulp. It is well to steam the pieces over boiling water in a large potato steamer for some ten minutes, then place in a large basin, cover with the weighed quantity of sugar, the lemon and ginger, and leave in a cool place overnight. Next day place in the preserving-pan and cook gently until the marrow becomes clear as amber and can be lifted out into jars. Boil up the syrup and strain to free it from ginger and peel, and pour over the contents of the jars tying down immediately. This makes a very nice confection.

Or :

The marrow after standing overnight, can be boiled down to a marmalade, the ginger and lemon being cut into shreds in the first instance and boiled with the fruit.

PLUM JAM

Egg Plums and Victorias make a rich and luscious jam but should be taken when just under-ripe.

They will bear rather more than their own weight of sugar, and it is well to boil the fruit first, remove as many stones as possible then, and the rest as completely as can be while the jam is finishing. The skins will partially dissolve if the fruit is at the right stage of under-ripeness ; if quite ripe there is a tendency for the skins to harden. From 20 to 30 minutes boiling after the sugar has been added is best.

Quince Jam

3-lbs. of quinces, slightly under-ripe ;
3½-lbs. sugar ;
1 lemon, juice only ;
3 pints water.

Peel, remove cores, and slice small, put into a pan with the water and cook rather slowly until soft and the fruit dissolving. Add the sugar and lemon-juice, and bring to boiling-point, boiling rather fast for 15 to 20 minutes. It should become almost clear and set well and should be a bright red colour.

By boiling the quinces before paring and coring, merely cutting them in quarters, adding the lemon-juice at same time as the water, straining when reduced to a soft pulp, and boiling some ten minutes only after sugar has been added, a fine jelly will result.

Raspberry Jam

3-lbs. picked raspberries ;
3-lbs. sugar ;
1 pint red currant juice.

Boil the fruit gently with the red currant juice until it is soft, but not a mash ; when at boiling-point add the heated sugar and when boiling-point is again reached continue for 10 minutes only.

RHUBARB JAM

> 3-lbs. red rhubarb weighed after cutting into inch-lengths.
> 2 lemons, juice only ;
> ¼-lb. stem ginger, well bruised.
> 2½-lbs. soft sugar.

Boil the rhubarb with the lemon-juice and ginger before adding the sugar ; when soft add the sugar, boil 15 minutes, remove the ginger and pot down.

Or boil longer to make it stiffer and darker in colour, adding mixed spices as well as ginger, and pot down in small pots for use as chutney.

STRAWBERRY JAM

> 3-lbs. small ripe red strawberries ;
> 1 pint red currant juice ;
> 3-lbs. sugar.

If red currant juice is not obtainable use the juice of 3 or 4 lemons, or a proportion of " Certo ", and rather less sugar.

If desired to keep the berries whole do not boil more than ten minutes from time sugar is added.

To prevent the berries rising in the jars let the jam cool down before putting into pots.

Gooseberry-juice will do instead of red currant if more convenient to obtain.

JAM FROM DRIED FRUITS
When using dried fruits, such as dried peaches,

apricots and pears, all of which make excellent jam, it is a good plan to include with them some tinned or fresh pineapple—the little brown South African pines which are sold quite cheap are most suitable, and combine remarkably well, too, with melon or marrow pulp, the flavour being further improved by adding lemon-juice during the later boiling.

Thus, when the fresh fruit crop gives but a poor yield we need not despair ; we have large resources open to us in imported fruits, and we can use these to increase our own, or instead of our own, at very small expense.

3. *Marmalades*

MARMALADES are made from Citrus fruits, and of these again we have a variety, thanks to increasing importation.

Bitter oranges are more frequently in use than the true Seville, and few people know the difference between them. In the true Seville orange the skin is bright as well as rough, and of a deep orange colour ; in the Bitter orange the skin is dull, rough, sometimes spotty, and the fruit is less well-shaped.

The addition of lemons, grapefruit, of Sweet or Jaffa oranges to bitter ones is purely a matter of taste ; some people like a combination ; others prefer the flavour of orange alone.

MARMALADE FOR HOUSEHOLD STOCK (Producing 30-lbs.)

1 large Grapefruit ;	12 Seville ;
2 lemons ;	12-lbs. sugar ;
2 Jaffa oranges ;	12 pints water.

Slice the fruit as thinly as possible or put through a mincing-machine or cutter, picking out the pips and covering these with water in a separate bowl. Measure the 12 pints of water and pour over the sliced fruit in the preserving-pan and leave to soak for 24 hours. Boil up without adding anything to it until the fruit looks transparent—for about one hour—and again set pan aside. Twenty-four hours later boil up again for half an hour, adding then the liquor obtained from straining the soaked pips through a colander. Put in the sugar and after it has dissolved boil the marmalade again for three-quarters of an hour or till it becomes transparent and of a deep golden colour, then fill the jars and tie down at once. If the jars are made hot in the oven there will be no danger of cracking, and the marmalade will set very quickly and be perfectly transparent.

The above is a recipe that has never failed to produce a marmalade of delicious flavour and firm quality, one that proves an excellent standby for regular household use throughout the year.

TRANSPARENT ORANGE MARMALADE (To produce 6-lbs.)

5 Seville oranges ;
1 Jaffa ;
5-lbs. fine sugar ;
3 pints of water.

Pare the yellow rind from the fruit as thinly as possible and cut into finest shreds or put through a mincer ; remove the white pith and chop this small, tying it in a muslin bag ; press out all the juice from the fruit and strain this till clear. Boil the pulp and the pith together in sufficient water to cover them, for about half an hour, to extract all the goodness from them. Strain this liquor through fine muslin and weigh it together with the pure juice, put into the preserving-pan and boil with the shredded peel until this is tender—about 15 minutes. Add the sugar and boil again for 30 minutes, then pour into clear glass jars made very hot and tie down with parchment.

GRAPEFRUIT MARMALADE (To produce 5-lbs.)

> 4 large ripe Grapefruit ;
> 2 lemons ;
> 3 pints of water ;
> ¼-oz. tartaric acid ;
> 4-lbs. sugar.

Slice all the fruit as thinly as possible, removing the pips ; put latter into separate basin and cover with water ; measure the three pints and cover the sliced fruit with this adding the tartaric acid. Next day simmer this, adding the strained water from the pips. Bring to boiling-point after simmering for an hour, add the sugar and boil again half an hour. Pour into hot jars and cover when cold.

LEMON JELLY MARMALADE

This is delicate, rather sharp in flavour, and is much liked by invalids.

> 12 juicy lemons ;
> 2-lbs. sugar ;
> 2 pints water.

Pare the rind as thinly as possible and mince very finely ; cut the fruit right through in pieces and press out all the juice into a bowl, straining to remove pips and pith. Measure the water and add to the juice with the minced rind. Boil gently for 20 minutes, then add sugar and after this is dissolved boil for a further 20 minutes and put into small glass jars. This marmalade should be very clear and delicate in appearance.

OTHER FRUIT MARMALADES

Dried Apricots, Peaches and Pears make very good marmalades, as also fresh Quinces, Marrows and Melons. If using dried fruits cut these first into fine shreds with a sharp knife as they cannot be so well handled after soaking, when using fresh fruit larger pieces will do, Soak dried fruits for a couple of days or even longer, before giving the first boiling ; add sugar when boiling up for a second time. Dried fruits will absorb nearly four times their own weight of water. Fresh quinces, marrows and melons should stand covered with sugar only for a day or so, then a small quantity of water can be added when boiling the fruit. Boil 30 or 40 minutes or till the marmalade looks clear. When using peaches, pines, melons and sweet fruits like nectarines, grapes, etc., it should be remembered that some acid such as lemon-juice will be required, or the addition of citric acid in powder-form. When making jams from sweet fruits of this type which are deficient in pectin it would be quite useful to add a small quantity of a product called " Certo " to the pulp, as this is a pure natural pectin and it ensures setting and keeping without in any way affecting the flavour of the jam.

Apple, Lemon and Ginger Marmalade

5-lbs. rough and sour apples ;
3 lemons, rind and juice ;
4-ozs. stem ginger ;
2 teaspoonfuls ground ginger ;
4-lbs. sugar ;
1 pint water.

Peel, remove cores, and cut up the apples into the preserving-pan, boil the peelings and cores in water by themselves, then strain over the apples. Cook until soft, add the lemon-juice and grated rind, the sugar and ground ginger, and stem ginger after chopping this fine. Boil again, stirring well, until it will set. 15 minutes should be sufficient, but more may improve it.

4. *Brandied Fruits for Dessert*

BRANDIED fruits are a somewhat old-fashioned type of preserve to which the spirit gives a unique flavour. To some extent they have been replaced by " Konfyts ", yet these are not by any means the same thing. Where spirit can be afforded Brandied Fruits will always be preferred.

BRANDIED PEACHES

Use equal quantities of fruit and sugar ;
To 4-lbs. weight of fruit use 1 pint of brandy.

Make a syrup with the sugar using just enough water to dissolve it, then bring this to boiling-point in a saucepan and put in the halved peaches, having removed the stones. Cook slowly so as not to break, and when quite tender lift the fruit into a jar and continue to boil the syrup for another twenty minutes or until it thickens well ; add the brandy at this stage and remove from the fire ; pour the hot liquid over the fruit and seal down at once.

The skins should be drawn off peaches before brandying, and if plums are being treated they should first be stoned and be pricked all over. Do not allow the fruit to break, or be spoiled in shape.

BRANDIED CHERRIES

Fill the bottle with freshly-picked Morella cherries. Make a syrup with a pound of sugar and half a pint of water for every 2 lbs. of fruit. Boil well and pour over the cherries when warm, but not hot. Leave a while, then turn into a saucepan and heat up slowly, not quite to boiling-point ; take out the fruit with a skimmer and fill the bottles ; boil the syrup and add brandy, and fill up to the neck, sealing at once.

Frosted Currants for Dessert

Pick fine large fruit when fully ripe ; wash well in water first, dry in the sun, then dip each bunch at a time in a mixture of frothed white of egg with a very little water stirred in. Drain until nearly dry and roll in powdered lump sugar. If not sufficiently coated the first time repeat the dip and roll again. Lay on white paper to dry. This makes a very pretty garnish for fruit jellies or custards, trifles and creams.

Cherries and Grapes can be frosted in the same way.

Candying of Fruits

While Candying of Fruits is an elaborate process and is hardly worth the while of the country housewife unless she is a capable maker of Sweetmeats, anyone who has gained a little practice in making clear syrup will find a field of original experiment open to her in making crystallised flowers.

Rose petals, violet petals, almond blossom, peach blossom, orange flowers, heliotrope, indeed almost any sweet-scented flower-petals can be crystallised by boiling, cooling, re-boiling and cooling and boiling yet again until the syrup candies and the petals are almost transparent. Practice makes perfect in this art. It is a pastime for those who like to make experiments ; but in the South of France it is a great industry.

5. *Fruit Juices, Cordials, etc.*

HESE can all be made by people who have any quantity of fruit of various kinds, and can be kept for an indefinite time if care is taken to seal the bottles thoroughly, and to sterilise them first. Fruit Juices, which are mainly used for sauce-making, are often bottled without sugar although they keep better if made into a syrup ; provided they are sealed and made air-tight, they will not ferment ; Fruit Syrups keep good for a longer time because of the sugar addition. Fruit Cordials are made with spirit as well as sugar and so keep an indefinite time.

The most suitable fruits for all such purposes are juicy and acid ones, such as Currants and Goosberries, but Raspberries, Loganberries and Blackberries answer very well. Fruit Wines, which are a different proposition, and about which there is a great deal more to be said, are made from a wide range of fruits and berries and from flowers like the Cowslip and Marigold and roots like the Parsnip.

Juices that are to be used for sauces, etc., are extracted from ripe fruit by pressure, not by boiling or pulping. It helps, however, to warm the fruit a little as to do so induces the juice to flow more freely, and a good method to follow is to place the picked and fully ripe fruit in a bowl that it does not more than three-parts fill, then to stand the bowl in the oven, covered with paper. Let it warm gradually but it should not become really hot. Crush it down from time to time, using a pestle or wooden spoon, until it seems as if all the juice had been extracted, then pour through a fine strainer into another bowl. Were sugar to be added at this stage the juice would form a cordial and if boiled up would make jelly ; as this is not the object, it is better to set the bowl in a cool place for three or four days so that the juice sharpens by beginning to ferment. Fermentation must not be allowed to go on, otherwise a vinegar would be formed, and when one is preserving juice for cooking purposes the object is to avoid making an acid as well as to avoid making a syrup.

To ensure good keeping the strained juice is put into bottles, which are well corked down, then placed in a deep pan of water, protected at the bottom, and gradually brought up to boiling-point. At this stage the bottles can be lifted out and the corks coated with melted sealing-wax. Leave to cool down, then label the bottles and put them away.

This pure fruit juice, being unsweetened and full of flavour, is of great service in making ices, pudding sauces, and for adding to curries and certain meat dishes.

Fruit Cordials, which are used for making drinks in company with soda water and lemonade, are another type of thing altogether. Properly speaking, they should be made with alcohol, but as that cannot be bought freely in Britain as it can be abroad, it is usually left out. Where spirit can be used it is poured over the picked ripe fruit and left under cover for some days, until it has drawn out not only all the flavour, but all the colour as well, and is then heated with sugar in sufficient amount to make a rich syrup. This is put into suitable bottles, corked and sealed, and sterilised for long keeping. A cheap brandy may be used in place of pure alcohol, but the crushed and strained fruit juice boiled with almost an equal weight of sugar, to which a little spirit is added before corking and sealing, is the usual method employed here for producing a Fruit Cordial. To sterilise the bottles is an advantage as this ensures their long keeping.

Black Currants, Raspberries and Blackberries, make the best and most useful Cordials. The fruits should be very fully ripe, very fine and juicy, and very free from stalks and seeds. An easy way of obtaining the juice is to rub the ripe fruit through a hair-sieve, but it will not be quite so clear as when crushed and strained, or as when extracted with the help of spirit.

6. *Home-made Wines and other Beverages*

QUITE a lengthy list of these could be made out, for country people have been used to brewing and wine-making for generations, and of late years there has been a renewal of interest in home-brewed drinks among the class that has more recently " discovered " the countryside by the help of the touring car and the camp, and by the thirsty " hiker ", to whom drinks of local character make a strong appeal. For the sake of this revived interest we have sought out and included herewith some old and tried recipes upon which a new generation may like to expend its energies.

The list given here by no means includes all old favourites, but it gives a choice and affords sufficient scope for all the spare energy a busy country housewife is likely to have to give to this branch of industry, and covers all, or nearly all, the " raw material " she is likely to have to deal with. For easy reference the recipes have been taken in alphabetical order, and therefore are not all, strictly speaking, wines, but " beverages " of various sorts. For instance, we begin with :

CHERRY BRANDY

This drink is the " standby " of the housekeeper of olden time, and usually made in July or August.

The Morella cherry is the best to use because it is acid ; but other sour cherries will do, providing they are quite fully ripe. Gather in dry weather and use very fresh. Wipe with a soft cloth and cut off the stalks, leaving about an inch-length on each cherry. Very lightly fill some wide-necked bottles after first weighing the fruit and setting aside three ounces of dry castor sugar to each pound. Prick the cherries with a needle and sprinkle the dry sugar over at intervals when filling the bottles. Fill up with good French brandy and cork tightly, covering the cork with melted sealing-wax. Set away and keep one or two months before using.

Some put one or two cloves in each bottle of cherries, and others add a few split almonds, but if the fruit is fine and well-flavoured it will need no other addition.

Cowslip Wine

Pick two quart measures of cowslip pips, i.e., the flowers alone.

Take 2-lbs. of loaf sugar, the
Rind and juice of one orange ;
Rind and juice of two lemons, and
2 quarts of water.

Boil sugar, water, rind and juice together for twenty minutes, and when only " new-milk warm " pour over the picked flowers. Stir well, and when a little settled put in a slice of bread spread with fresh brewers' yeast. Leave for a day, then strain into a small cask that has held brandy ; bung it well and keep six or seven weeks before using.

Currant Wine

Pick, stem and rub fresh and very ripe currants through a sieve ; they can be all red, all black, or mixed.

To each quart of strained juice add
1-lb. castor sugar ;
½ pint water (cold).

Stir well until sugar is perfectly dissolved, then leave

in a tub or cask, covered with muslin, to ferment. Do not put into bottles until all fermentation has ceased, which will be in about a fortnight's time. Cork well and seal down.

DAMSON WINE

Use only sound and ripe fruit ; pick off stalks. Weigh the fruit and allow to each pound of damsons one pint of boiling water.

Pour water over the fruit in a stone jar and leave four or five days, stirring every day.

Strain off the liquor pressing goodness out of fruit with a wooden spoon ; add to each quart a pound of lump sugar, stir until dissolved, then put into a wooden cask and add a pint of brandy to each six quarts of liquor. Keep several months before using or drawing off into bottles.

DANDELION WINE

Pick a quart measure of yellow petals and put into a tub or pippin and pour over enough boiling water to cover. Leave for three days, but stir frequently in meantime.

Strain the liquid and put on to boil with the rind of one lemon and one orange, thinly peeled, and one pound of lump sugar to each quart of liquid.

Strain into a deep bowl and place an ounce of dried yeast, or a slice of toast spread with brewers' yeast, on the top.

Leave for three or four days, then strain again and bottle the wine in the usual way.

This wine is very good for people troubled with liver complaints.

ELDERBERRY WINE
8-lbs. of picked berries ;
8 pints of boiling water ;
4-lbs. lump sugar to 5 quarts of liquor ;
1-oz. powdered cinnamon ;
½-oz. powdered cloves.

Put picked berries into a tub, pour the boiling water over them, adding a little more than the quantity stated if they are not well covered. Leave for a day at least, stirring and pressing the berries from time to time.

Strain through a sieve, pressing the berries with a large wooden spoon or masher to extract all the juice.

Measure the liquor yielded and put into a deep pan with the sugar and spices ; boil fifteen minutes ; pour into a deep stone jar and throw a cloth lightly over it. When cool put a portion of dried yeast on the top, about 2 ozs. When it has ceased fermenting skim carefully and then bottle it, leaving 2 inches space at top of each bottle. Cork well and seal.

GRAPE WINE
Pick the grapes before they are fully ripe, and out-door-grown grapes are excellent for the purpose.

Put stalks and fruit (but no leaves or twigs), into a scrupulously clean tub, and bruise very thoroughly, adding an equal quantity of water. Leave for three days, stirring and pressing frequently. Strain off and to each quart of liquid add half a pound of lump sugar. Stir until dissolved then pour into a cask, which it should fill completely. Leave ten days to ferment, then pour in as much brandy as the cask will now hold to fill it up, and cork closely, letting cask stand in a cool place. Leave in the cask until the vines begin to bud again, then it is ready to bottle off and should eventually be sparkling as champagne.

Hop and Sherry Cordial

Fill wide-mouthed bottles with ripe hops as full as they will hold, by pressing down ; cover them with light sherry and let them infuse for a month. Strain then and add an equal amount of clear syrup from boiled sugar and water. Mix well and keep in corked bottles. A small measure of this taken with water makes a beneficial drink.

Hop and Malt Beer

The making of these is a lengthy and elaborate process and requires the proper tubs and coppers for the purpose, but some country people make a small quantity of home-brewed beer from fresh hops, boiled in water, using yeast for fermenting it. The difficulty, is to get the right heat and this is where the housewife who uses a thermometer has an advantage.

The degree of heat which the water used should reach is 170 degrees.

The malt grains are mashed with water at this heat. After being crushed they are left to stand two hours, then the liquor is carefully drawn off and added to the liquor from the hops which are strained out and after cooling down to 70 degrees this is left to " work " in a tub with a sack thrown over the top. It should stand in a warm place, and in about six or eight hours will start to show a froth which will keep on rising for another forty-eight hours. This should be skimmed off at intervals. When the liquor ceases to work any more it is poured into a cask and bunged up. No air must get into it. Keep some time before drawing off.

MEAD

This is a simple beverage seldom made by any but the cottager who keeps bees. After most of the honey has been taken from a hive the bee-keeper dissolves what is left in as much water as is needed to do this, then boils it and skims well. The combs are also boiled in water so that nothing is lost. The liquor is left undisturbed for two or three days, then has a little fresh yeast added to it, and a little ginger, cloves, cinnamon and mace, and a few sprigs of rosemary. It is put into a tub while the yeast works, then is drawn off clear and kept some months before using.

NETTLE BEER

Gather a good quantity of young nettles and boil with sufficient water to cover them well, and after some minutes strain off clear from the pulp.

To each quart of strained liquor add

1-oz. ground ginger ;
$\frac{1}{2}$-oz. cream of tartar ;
Juice of a lemon ;
$\frac{1}{2}$-lb. lump sugar.

Boil again five minutes, leave to cool, strain clear, stir in a little dried yeast and let ferment overnight. Next morning strain clear and bottle for use.

QUINCE WINE

This is made by mixing one quart of the strained juice of quinces obtained by quartering the fruit and boiling it with water for about an hour. There should be sufficient water to cover the fruit and allow it to float. To a quart of juice allow one pound of lump sugar, boil till clear, then allow to ferment for two or three days.　Add a gill of brandy and put up in well-corked bottles.

Raspberry Vinegar

Put ripe raspberries, as many as can be obtained, into a stone pippin and mash them to a pulp.　Pour over sufficient white wine vinegar to cover well (use the best vinegar obtainable).　Stand in the sun all day and leave a night in a cool place ; it is well to give an occasional stir.　Next day strain off, return the liquid to the jar and put in as many more fresh raspberries as before, mash and again set in the sun all day.　Strain again the second day and this time to each quart of liquid add

> 1 pint of water ;
> 2-lbs. best white sugar.

Place over a fire and stir until the sugar is all dissolved ; bring very slowly up to boiling-point, remove any scum and strain into a jug.　Put into a bottle while still warm and cork well, running melted sealing-wax over the top.

(A spoonful at the bottom of a tumbler filled up with soda water makes a most refreshing drink.)

Strawberry Sherbet

(A refreshing drink for Tennis Parties.)

> 1-lb. very ripe strawberries ;
> 1 lemon, juice only ;
> 1 pint water ;
> 1 tablespoonful brandy ;
> ¼-lb. castor sugar.

Crush the strawberries to a paste, add all the other

ingredients except the sugar, and leave to stand three hours ; stir and strain over the sugar in a jug ; stir again and set away on ice to cool or in cold place for a couple of hours ; when using place a little at the bottom of each glass and fill up with soda water.

Sherry Cobbler

> Some slices of fresh or tinned pineapple ;
> One lemon thinly sliced ;
> One orange thinly sliced ;
> Small teacupful of powdered sugar ;
> Wineglassful of Sherry ;
> Pounded ice if obtainable ;
> Some water.

Use a wide-mouthed glass jug and lay the fruit at the bottom, sprinkling the sugar over ; cover with the ice and leave ten minutes ; when dissolved pour in the wine and some water, stir up thoroughly, then leave to settle before pouring into glasses. A slice of fruit should be served with each glass, and it should be sucked through straws.

Rhubarb Wine

Cut five pounds of rhubarb into short lengths, bruise and chop it and put into a deep bowl with about a gallon of cold water. Leave for five days, stirring occasionally. Strain off the liquor and add to it three pounds of lump sugar and stir until dissolved. Put in the peeled rind of two lemons, the yellow part only, and an ounce of isinglass. Leave to ferment five days, then skim carefully, draw off the liquor into a small cask and leave unstopped for about a fortnight. Then close up and begin to use the wine in about six months' time. If the colour has seemed poor deepen it with a little currant juice.

SLOE WINE

Pick sloes which are sound and ripe ; reject all that are bruised and decayed. Pick off the stalks, put them into a deep pan and pour over an equal quantity of boiling water, i.e., a gallon of water to a gallon of sloes. Leave to steep for five days, stirring frequently. Strain off the liquor and allow four pounds of lump sugar to a gallon of that. Bring to the boil then cool down, and when cold put into a small cask with a pint of brandy or gin. Keep in the cask twelve months before bottling.

MANGEL-WURZEL WINE

If good whisky is obtained from potatoes, a wine almost as strong and heady is obtained from mangels.

Thoroughly wash and scrub clean, but do not peel, enough mangels to make ten pounds' weight when cut in slices. Add one ounce of dried hops and 2 ozs. of root ginger well bruised. Boil with water sufficient to cover well for two hours. Strain through a sieve or bag, add more water to make up a gallon, then put in 2 lbs. brown sugar and stir until dissolved. When cool put in an ounce of dried yeast and leave to ferment in open cask. When fermentation ceases skim well, put in a bunch of dried raisins, cork well and keep six months before using.

(It will be noticed that a small cask is advised in the case of nearly all home-made wines, and this should be procured if at all possible. It is not easy to find any substitute for it, as fermentation is apt to break bottles and a tub gives too much surface exposure.)

EASILY-MADE FRUIT WINE—BLACKBERRY, DAMSON OR APPLE

To every quart of ripe, sound whole fruit allow one quart of boiling water. Keep in a stone pippin and stir up every day for a fortnight, then strain, and add 1 lb. of sugar to every quart of liquor, with a morsel of bruised ginger and blade of mace. Keep in a warm place and skim every day for another fortnight, then strain again and put into bottles. Leave the corks loosely inserted until fermentation is quite finished, then screw down tight and set away. Keep six months.

7. *Making Fruit Pulp—A Temporary Means of Preserving*

EOPLE who go to the country at week-ends are sometimes puzzled to know how to save small quantities of fruit that have ripened sooner than they expected, for which they have made no provision of jars or sugar, yet wish to save until such time as they can deal with it in proper fashion. Pulping is a very suitable method of accumulating small amounts, as well as a method that is much used by growers of large crops, who find it saves carriage to send consignments of fruit to their customers in this way—foreign growers send much fruit from their fields to our jam factories by this means. In fruit-growing districts pulping machinery will be found in fairly general use, sometimes actually on the field itself, while in other places there are factories that carry out this preliminary process but do not turn out the finished product. The housewife at home can do the same on as small a scale as she pleases and find it equally advantageous as a temporary measure of preservation.

Pulped fruit will not keep indefinitely, of course ; but it will keep sweet for a considerable time if stored in an air-tight container in a cool place. The best type of container is a wooden tub or enamelled can with close-fitting cover, or any sort of jar that it is possible to keep closely sealed up. Anyone who has watched the dispatch of a large cargo of fruit pulp from a Normandy port will have noticed that small wooden casks seem to be the type of container generally used.

The wooden tub may not be available in the small house, but a large metal container with close-fitting lid such as is used for holding sweets in big quantities may sometimes be had from a village shop. Better still is it to store the fruit pulp in bottles with glass tops and metal clips such as would be used for the proper bottling method ; if these are filled and then sterilised for an hour or so, the pulp so stored may be expected to keep an indefinite time.

How to Make Fruit Pulp

Reject any defective or spoilt fruit, pick over the good, cleanse it by washing and remove stems, then put into a large pan or clean saucepan with a little water at the bottom to prevent burning. Cover and let it cook over gentle heat, stirring occasionally. When done in large quantities coppers or vats are used, or special machinery made for the purpose. Pulp should be thoroughly but slowly cooked and when reduced to a uniform mass it can be put into holders and sealed up immediately. Sealing in the ordinary fruit bottle, as we have said, presents no difficulty, but where a tub or cask or stone jar has to be used it is another matter. A covering of melted suet is quite good, especially if stout paper is tied over the top later ; but containers with lids that fit them should be used by people who make pulp in quantities.

The largest amount of fruit pulp is made from plums and early apples. Plums ripen quickly and fall readily and there is not always the convenience for using them at once, so the pulping method is adopted to save the few or many from being wasted. Early apples and windfalls, neither of which will keep well, are also admirably suited for making pulp that can, in its turn, become the foundation of Apple Butter, Apple Amber, Apple Sauce, and be used for tarts and charlottes, or with other acid fruits such as cranberries and bilberries and blackberries, to soften their astringency. Many and varied are the uses that can be found for Apple Pulp, as many indeed as those for Tomato Pulp (the Pulping Method being ideal for safe storing of the surplus tomato crop), while Plum Pulp is the foundation of many jams that go under other labels—and are none the worse for doing so !

PULPING VEGETABLES

The Pulp Method is also extremely useful for making a store or saving a crop of Spinach or Sorrel. It is a common practice among French householders to keep a store of pulped Sorrel, usually in a deep stone pippin, for use during the winter months. It is wanted for making soups and those delicious *purées* served with veal and other meats. In England we store Spinach in the same way or perhaps more often in jars hermetically-sealed—Bottled Spinach being quite one of the best among the list of vegetables that it pays to preserve after this manner.

WHEN USING PULP

When ready to use fruit pulp for the purpose of making Jam the jars should be opened and the pulp put through a strainer before it goes into the preserving-pan. As weighing will be somewhat difficult with a product of this kind it will be advisable to weigh the pan first, then again after the pulp is in ; do not more than half-fill the pan at any time.

As it is being heated the pulp will need frequent stirring to prevent catching at the bottom of the pan, and again it may be mentioned how advisable it is to use spoons that are cut in a slant, to ensure clearing the bottom.

As the pulp boils it will lose the dull and cloudy appearance it had, and after sugar has been added and it has boiled clear there will be little difference between the conserve made from fresh fruit and that made from this pulp. After boiling with sugar it can be put into ordinary jam jars and covered with paper in the usual way.

8. *Storage of Fruit*

THE loss that sometimes occurs when Apples and Pears are put by in store shows that unsuitable places for keeping are often to blame and that it pays to provide the right type of keeping-place if this can be done.

Many people lay out their fruit on straw on shelves or the floor of a storeroom or attic and are surprised to find how badly it keeps. Straw is one of the last things to be used, and the attic is subject to changes of weather, being sometimes too hot and sometimes too cold. The better place is a cool cellar partly underground and shelves formed of wooden slats that allow air to reach the fruit. A still better keeping-place is a pit or a fruit-room that is partly sunk in the earth and roofed over, in which the temperature will be kept as nearly even as can be, frost being prevented from entering by a thatch of straw. If kept in the shade or dark and in an even temperature, fruit will ripen very slowly and decay will as slowly show itself.

Wherever kept, pears and apples should be scanned every week and signs of decay in any specimen should mean the instant removal of the offender. If only slightly affected this can be used for cooking or in some other mode. Pears that ripen late keep very well in drawers or chests between folds of rugs, and it is not at all a bad plan to wrap fine fruit in soft tissue-paper before putting away.

It would seem that any fruit stored in a dry, clean place ought to keep perfectly well without having recourse to any of the methods of preservation that

have just been considered. Why is that not the case ?
Why is it necessary to " preserve " it ?

A considerable amount of fruit is kept in a natural
state by every householder who has an orchard yielding
tree-fruit, but apart from that it is possible to keep
hardly any of the softer kind such as bush or plant-
fruit, and even tree-fruit will keep for only a limited
period. The reason is that fruits and vegetables, like
ourselves, are subject to the great law of change that
means a continuous process of building up and breaking down, of growth and decay. Even our methods
of preserving merely arrest the process ; they do not
prevent changes taking place in course of time.

The chief causes of deterioration in products like
fruits and vegetables is mainly bacterial, however.
The air holds multitudes of micro-organisms that are
only to be detected by the microscope yet are very
surely present, and their mission is to break down the
constituent elements of plant and animal life and make
possible their re-absorption into other elements needful
for human life. This continual process leads to decay
as well as to re-formation under other processes. By
preserving we arrest a process ; we do not ultimately
prevent it.

Where means are not taken to arrest decay this is
liable to begin quite soon after a crop of any type has
come to maturity, but when we want to keep anything
without preserving by cooking or other methods we
gather it before it is full ripe, keep it from the atmosphere and in the dark, but even then can only arrest
decay for a time.

Hard fruits like apples and pears that carry on their
ripening for some time after they are gathered can be
kept fairly well if laid on open shelves, or a dry floor,

in a cool dry place, whether loft or cellar. Even so it is necessary to keep a watch over them, and remove any that show signs of decay from contact with the rest. Apples that have a tendency to " sweat " need constant looking over ; this is no detriment to them and often prevents the shrinking that other kinds undergo ; but they should be kept on open shelves and as far as may be from touching each other. Sour apples or the good-keeping variety of cooking fruit can be kept in barrels of chaff or sawdust with advantage. Sweet dessert apples may be helped by keeping them wrapped in soft papers and away from the light. In trying to keep a lot together it is inevitable that some will decay, therefore careful sorting at first is good economy, when such as are not likely to keep in a natural state may be saved by drying or by pulping or by " preserving " in some fashion. Pears that will assuredly not keep long should be bottled or canned, or even dried in good time.

PRESERVATION BY CANNING

Preservation of Fruits and Vegetables by the Canning Method does not usually come into the country housewife's range of possibilities, and is less likely to do so as the number of firms who put up all kinds of produce in this way increases year by year. Canning on a small scale is too costly and too difficult for it to be generally adopted, and the need for experimenting grows less as time goes on. The spread of the Canning Industry is to be welcomed rather than deprecated, especially in Great Britain, for it means the increasing cultivation of larger and better crops of many kinds, increased employment possibilities in rural districts where formerly it was becoming difficult to earn a livelihood, and best of all it brings a large supply of varied food within the range of the small income, which makes for health, adds to pleasure, and so is a benefit to everyone.

The purpose of preservation by Canning is for the sake of keeping food for a longer time than it can be kept by almost any other method. When canning methods are perfect they can be depended upon for years and enable the product to be transported anywhere. Canning can be successful, carried out in a small way on a small property, but it needs the scientific treatment and the proper equipment of the modern factory for success to be guaranteed. As it has developed into a wonderful industry and has led to extensive fruit- and vegetable-growing in places where corn-growing was becoming unprofitable it is to be acclaimed as a welcome addition to the country's resources and that is all the more reason why the small grower is well advised not to attempt this method at home, but to preserve small crops in other ways, of which there is a quite sufficient variety to satisfy all who wish to experiment.

Methods of Storing Vegetables are given in the section devoted to Vegetable Preservation.

9. *Preserving Fruit and Vegetables by Drying or Evaporation*

THIS simple method of keeping and storing both Fruit and Vegetable produce is far too little practised among British growers, partly, perhaps, because it is so much better carried out by Overseas producers, with their greater facilities for drying in the open, whereas in this climate it has to be done by artificial heat, nevertheless, it is a method that is of great use in times of emergency, and one that is both reliable and successful when carried on in the home on a small scale as well as in the factory on a larger one. At one period, during the Great War, a large amount of drying was done, and it proved of great service at home also providing a good deal of useful food for the Army. By this means private people saved much food from being wasted when there were few facilities for preserving it in any other way.

There are seasons when an unusually plentiful crop of orchard fruit makes drying the most suitable method of dealing with it because much of it falls early and will not keep long. There are Vegetables, too, that cannot be Bottled or Pickled or otherwise preserved because of a lack of room, and drying comes in as an excellent method of disposing of large quantities, as after evaporation the produce takes up so little space.

No elaborate machinery is necessary, although there are Evaporators on the market which do the work very effectively.

When drying at home, on a small scale, it is sufficient to make one or two Trays by nailing together four strips of wood to form a square, and tacking a piece of hessian or coarse cloth between. Such trays would be needed when the drying is carried on out of doors in the sun, also when it is done in a greenhouse, as these trays are convenient for carrying to and fro. But even trays are not necessary when drying is done indoors in the oven, as then it is sufficient to lay sheets of thick blotting-paper on the shelves of the oven or on the top of a range when the fire has gone down. If using a gas oven and keeping on a light, let this be turned very low indeed.

Warmth and Air for Drying Fruit

The essential thing to keep in mind is that air is as necessary as heat when preserving by Evaporation. That is why, in warm climates, drying is always done in the open. We are drying-out the moisture or water that is in the fruit or vegetable, as it is that which causes decay, but nothing else is changed, and therefore, when the moisture is restored by soaking, it returns to its original size and shape, flavour and character.

When using the oven for drying the door must be left ajar for air to enter and for any steam that may be created to escape. In the Evaporators there is provision for a free circulation of air to be maintained all the time the machine is in work.

Whatever material, fruit or vegetable, is to be dried, should be cleaned, trimmed, cut in slices or shreds, and spread in a rather thin layer over the sheets of paper or trays. If drying Apples, for instance, which may be fallings, they should be wiped clean, pared, cored and sliced, not too thinly, and so spread out to dry. It may be that some apples have been eaten by grubs

81 F

on one side, but the other half is quite sound ; in this case cut away the spoilt portion, pare and trim the rest. When describing the way to do this to an audience of country folk, a lecturer was highly amused to hear an old lady ask to have the directions repeated as she had not quite grasped what should be done to " apples that are not very well ".

Apples can also be dried whole, by paring, coring, and stringing them on skewers or thin wooden rods which can be lodged on supports in the oven, or have a string run through them and be dried in a warm room. In this way they shrink and shrivel and look like balls of leather, yet when soaked come back to their original size and shape in a most amazing fashion.

The white rings of dried apple which we buy from Overseas producers have been blanched before drying to keep them from discolouration, and the home-dryer may blanch her own by sulphuring them first. As whiteness is not really essential, it need not be considered any sign of deterioration when the drying apple portions become brown.

In our climate there is no fruit that pays so well for drying as the Apple, but Pears can be kept from deterioration by the same means, and they, too, can be blanched by sulphuring them first. Plums also dry well, and Grapes, but the result is not Prunes, nor yet Raisins, as much more goes to the production of these choice fruits than mere evaporation. In Britain we seldom have any overplus of fruit other than the apple, therefore it is sufficient to our purpose to describe how to deal with that.

To Blanch Apples and Pears

Before the fruit is pared and cored and cut in rings

or slices, a number of jars should be got ready for filling with sulphur fumes. Use 2 lb. jars (glass ones) by preference, and turn them upside down on a table. Fill an old iron spoon with powdered sulphur, set it alight, then insert this under each jar, removing it from one as soon as that is filled with the smoke and putting it under another. A number can be filled before the sulphur fumes are exhausted. As the first jar is filled reverse it and quickly drop into it several rings and put a plate on the top, then do the same with the rest, so using up all the rings. Shake the jars to move the rings about, and then take out the apples as the smoke fades away, put the rings on rods or strings as before described, and keep in a cool oven or in the sun until they feel dry and have a toughness like leather. " Leathery " is indeed the right description to apply to all evaporated fruit or vegetable produce after it has been sufficiently dried. If it is hard and brittle it is spoilt, for it will not then take up water when put to soak. When of the right texture, soaking for quite a short time restores both colour and shape, and, needless to say, the flavour remains unaltered.

Pears should be sulphured after they have been made ready in the same way as described for apples, but they take much longer to dry out their natural moisture, and a little longer to soak before cooking.

Fruit for drying should be fully developed and approaching ripeness, but not over-ripe. If it is " far gone " it will tend to cook and become soft when warmth is supplied.

We remind ourselves that drying by heat, generally sun-heat, has been a method of preserving everything from the earliest times, and sun-dried fruits, vegetables, herbs and seeds are still the mainstay of life during the winter season for large numbers of people. Modern methods have improved the appearance and extended the choice and given us new forms of dried food, and drying has become a great industry, especially in our own Overseas Dominions, so that no book that deals with the preservation of crops from orchard or garden would be complete unless the drying method was included in it. Nevertheless, for most housewives, drying will be applied to orchard fruits alone—apples and pears in particular.

To Store dried Fruits we keep them in bags or boxes, but not in tins ; it is well to let the air reach them to some extent, and not to put them into anything that is air-tight.

When making use of them soak in warm water for some hours, for although they quickly regain their original size and texture a longer time improves the quality. Soaking for a day or two is no detriment, and when making jam of dried apricots or other fruits soaking for two or three days is desirable.

. . . .

A few general directions in regard to preserving Vegetables by the Drying Method may come into this section as the method to be followed is almost precisely the same and we want to avoid unnecessary repetition.

Almost any Vegetable will dry well, although the usual method is to dry peas and haricots and lentils, and not much else. But where storage space is limited drying provides an easy and suitable and cleanly way of storing root vegetables such as carrots and onions, while among greens cabbage in shreds, leeks also shredded, and even spinach, become perfectly suitable for storing in small compass after treatment by drying. It must again be emphasised that nothing is lost but water, and that when this is restored the vegetable regains all its old values and to a large extent its original appearance.

GREEN BEANS

Many people preserve Runner Beans for winter use by putting them into a brine, whereas they are far easier to keep by the Drying Method. They should be gathered before they grow tough, be shredded as if for immediate cooking, and then spread out on trays or sheets of blotting-paper and dried in a cool oven with air admitted. They will shrivel and eventually look like wisps of dried hay, but when soaked over-night in water they return to their original crispness and colour and can then be cooked as if they had just been picked.

GREEN PEAS

These are sometimes left to dry in their pods, and where there is a warm dry shed in which to keep them this is not at all a bad plan, but is more trouble when they are wanted for cooking. If shelled and dried by gentle warmth and air, they will take up water again and after soaking will cook quite quickly and be found to possess all their original flavour.

GREEN VEGETABLES

Cabbage should be finely shred before drying and only the tender hearts should be used. Here again the colour vanishes, as with green beans, but it returns by soaking and by cooking in the usual way. Leeks should be carefully cleansed and shred across in slices, cut as fine as possible. Onions are skinned and shred very finely, and few things pay better for drying or are more useful when done. A small amount of dried onion suffices to give flavour to a soup or stew, and goes as far in effect as double the amount of fresh onion would do.

CARROTS

Carrots are most successful. Sometimes they are finely shred and mixed with other vegetables, but when done alone are pared and cut across in thin slices. After drying they shrivel and look sadly disappointing ; but when thrown into a bowl of water they begin to swell and recover colour, and in a remarkably short time will have returned to their original condition. Parsnips dry fairly well, too, but turnips do not keep their flavour and are apt to acquire a disagreeable taste.

While drying may not commend itself as a method of storage where vegetables are concerned, as there are other methods available which perhaps give less trouble, it is, all the same, strongly to be recommended for people who want to keep the produce of an allotment and who have only limited accommodation. The produce of a whole plot, when dried, can be stored in small boxes a cupboard or a few bags, and can be kept for an almost indefinite length of time without deteriorating.

GARDEN VEGETABLE PRODUCE

A CRISP SAVOY

III

1. *Small Crops with more Variety*

HEN the vegetable plots are studied from the point of view of the one who has to use their produce for cooking and storing, they are seen to offer possibilities such as the ordinary gardener can rarely visualise. She will want small crops with more variety and opportunity to make frequent changes in her bill of fare, a chance to make experiment and try new modes. No housekeeper who values her reputation as cook likes to be compelled to serve cauliflowers day after day simply because cauliflowers are " crying out " to be eaten, or to put spinach on the bill of fare because it is fast running to seed. On the other hand, she may sometimes search the garden over for herbs and flavourings, or some special plant or root that she particularly desires, and find it not ; or discover there is nothing wherewith to make a salad just when she most wishes to set one on the table !

The fact is that a kitchen garden—or a mere allotment, for the matter of that—should be considered from the cook's point of view first, rather than judged by the gardener's eye. The cook is guided by taste and by the appearance of things when they come on the table, while the gardener considers the show they make on the ground. Her judgment, surely, is more likely to be correct, for vegetables, unlike fruit and flowers, are grown solely for use.

A kitchen garden or a collection of plots devoted to growing vegetables may have a beauty of its own all the same. Strict utilitarianism need not rob it of interest or artistry. Take Marrows, for example :

Marrows over an Arch

Many gardeners plant marrows to hide a rubbish-heap or put them in some corner, leaving them to straggle at will, whereas this plant is a vine and wants to climb and an opportunity to let its fruit hang down like the grape. Give a marrow plant leave to climb and spread and it will cover an arch in the most decorative manner while it will produce the finest fruit it knows how if this can hang from a supporting trellis or pole.

Decorative Foliage

Things grown solely for use are often quite as decorative as others that are grown for their beauty alone and a kitchen garden is only unattractive when it is slovenly in its keeping and overcrowded. Some vegetables produce very beautiful foliage, like the deep reds and bronzes of beets or the bright grass-like green of salsify. A mistake too commonly made is to grow far too many straggling and ungainly specimens of Brussels sprouts or giant cabbages, and too few handsome curly kale or crisp savoys.

. . . .

A country housewife's garden should have in it uncommon vegetables, such, for instance, as :

Sorrel for Soups

Sorrel conserved in the form of Pulp has been mentioned before, but it may be remarked here that one or two rows of sorrel once sown from seed will come up

year after year and provide all the green leafage required by those who love Sorrel Soup and that delicious
purée sometimes served with veal or pork or sausage.

CHIVES

A plant of Chives, set in a border will give that
refined type of onion flavouring most suited to green
salads, most appropriate in stuffing mixtures and very
pleasant in sauces. It is the best to use for giving
savour to rissoles and omelets and delicious compo-
sitions of that kind.

CORN SALAD

This is a salad plant that is usually grown in cool
frames or in boxes under the staging in a greenhouse,
as it comes in the winter to replace lettuces and endive
and while without the usual crispness of salad greens
it is of pleasant flavour and very likeable.

SALSIFY

Another vegetable for winter use, of which we see
far too little grown. It has handsome foliage, so looks
well when growing in a bed, and has long tapering
roots that go far into the soil. It is the root that is so
pleasant to eat, and that when scraped and boiled
makes so good a dish to serve either under white sauce
or, better still, as fried, after being coated with egg and
crumbs, for the winter supper-table.

THE PEACH TOMATO

Few people, again, grow the Peach Tomato, the
kind that is seedless, is firm inside and has a lovely
flavour. Those who once have tried it will want no
other, for it is so pleasant to eat and travels so well, and

serves all manner of uses so much better than the ordinary kind.

CANADIAN WONDER BEANS

Then there is the long, straight tender bean, known as the " Canadian Wonder ", which when it appears on the market is invariably priced much higher than the common Scarlet Runner, and is worth it, too. This may as well be grown as any commoner kind, for it is no more trouble, and its long pods with their delicate white bean are so profitable to use that if the seed is a little more expensive it still is cheaper in the end.

GLOBE ARTICHOKES

A few plants of the Globe variety ought to be grown as well as a bed of the kind we call the Jerusalem artichoke. The green artichoke makes such a delicate and uncommon supper dish in summer and autumn, for eating either hot or cold, that it is deservedly considered a dish for epicures, yet everybody may enjoy it if they will. The root of the Globe artichoke bottles well and in that form is used for *entrées* and savouries.

CHINESE ARTICHOKES

One finds these in French markets under the name of *Crosnes*. This, too, is a hardy perennial, with tuberous root, and makes a welcome addition to winter vegetables. It wants good soil and some attention in order to make its best growth, and does well in light soil, enriched with a little manure. Its curious and fascinating roots rarely grow longer than 18 inches, but the small tubers should be planted in early spring in drills some few inches apart. They form in July and August and need then a little liquid manure, and as the plants have a tendency to make small side shoots these should be pinched off to encourage the development of main tubers. Usually one lifts these in November and then they are stored in sand in a shed, but they should not be allowed to become dry or shrivelled, which happens if lifted too early and too warmly stored.

Chinese artichokes are delicious if merely washed and dried, then fried in boiling fat to make slightly brown and served on buttered toast ; or they can be boiled and served with melted butter, with a sprinkling of dried cheese over.

CELERIAC

Here is another root that few people know anything about unless they are cooks with an experimental turn of mind, and then they know it well and appreciate it fully. It is the " turnip-rooted celery ", and it grows well in certain soils, and should be fed with liquid manure ; it reaches the size of a large turnip, and its rough, rather horny skin is no indication of its delicate, nutty flavour. This is yet one more of several vegetables that will make delicious dishes to serve alone with a sauce, or for baking after it has been boiled and sliced and covered with cheese. It is also excellent to serve with boiled turkey, roast mutton, and sausages.

BROCOLI

Purple Brocoli is fairly well known, but is not as freely cultivated by small growers as it should be, for it comes in so usefully in the early months of the year, when other greens are becoming scarce, and is sweet of flavour. Every housewife will want to have a few plants of brocoli put with curly kale and savoys in her cabbage patch.

GREEN MINT UNDER BELL CLOCHES

Take the precaution in early autumn of putting a good root of Mint under a bell cloche or in a cool frame, and then you will have a vigorous growth of young shoots in the early spring, long before any appears above ground—and how useful and acceptable it is just then!

GOOD KING HENRY OR MERCURY

This is one of the easiest things to grow and in Lincolnshire is a great favourite, where it is known as " Lincoln Asparagus ", but outside the Eastern Counties it is rarely met with. It is a perennial and a few rows once sown will come up season after season. It resembles spinach in appearance and is used in the same way, but is earlier in season and less bitter in flavour—Mercury makes, in fact, a very pleasant and useful dish of "greens" in spring just when other things are lacking. It is in season from March to June, just before ordinary spinach is ready to cut in most gardens. It repays having good soil and a warm border or bed.

To cook it treat exactly like spinach, using a little water first, but after draining and chopping cook again with butter and seasoning.

NEW ZEALAND SPINACH

This is a kind of Spinach that comes to its best when the ordinary kind is failing because the season has become too *hot* ! Originally imported from New Zealand as its name implies, it likes a hot dry soil. It is used in the same way as the ordinary kind when required for a dish, but its juice is valuable for colouring purposes in sweet-making and confectionery.

CARDOONS

The Cardoon is related to the Globe artichoke, and is more generally found in foreign markets, but is well worth cultivating in a cook's garden. It has a large fleshy leaf-stalk so that it also resembles Celery, and like celery should be blanched by earthing up. Like celery, too, it can be cooked in a variety of ways, but unlike celery is not good to eat raw. Some varieties have very sharp spines and are therefore objectionable in a garden and difficult to handle, but there are spineless sorts, the " Marseilles " variety is one, and this is fleshy and cooks easily. It is well to sow seeds in pots and plant out in trenches in May, planting some distance apart. Moisture is needed later, in fact, treatment similar to celery. For eating it is in season from September to March.

To cook cardoons they should be washed and the stems cut into short lengths, then boiled in salted water until the rough outside can be rubbed off with a cloth ; cool them in cold water, scrape well then put into a stewpan with strips of bacon, seasoning and a bunch of herbs ; simmer till tender and serve with the sauce slightly thickened.

2. How to Bottle Vegetables

THERE is not the same need to make a store of Bottled Vegetables as there is for preserving fruit in this way because the practice of canning has grown to such an extent of late years that it gives us perfectly preserved greens and roots for use all the year round. Nevertheless where there are good crops in the garden it is a matter of pride and satisfaction to be able to show a little store of bottled vegetables as well as of fruit and, after all, country folk are not always able to buy canned peas and beans with the same ease that townspeople may do.

Vegetables are more difficult to bottle successfully than any kind of fruit, and for that reason are avoided by people who cannot give the time and attention that is needed, but on the other hand, they are something of an achievement, and having once made a success of what is difficult to do we want to go on from better to best !

The reason why they are more difficult to conserve in this way is because they have little or none of the acid property that helps so much the preservation of fruit, and they need preservatives like salt and vinegar to take the place of this as well as greater heat to ensure their keeping.

PREPARING VEGETABLES FOR BOTTLING

Very careful preparation is necessary. First, the vegetables—carrots, peas, beans, celery or asparagus, etc., must be *young* and very freshly gathered, then most thoroughly cleansed, using a little salt in the water in the final rinsing. They should then be *blanched*, by boiling or steaming them for a few minutes to brighten the colour as well as to help the preservation, this also shrinks and makes them more pliable, as it does in the case of hard fruit like apples and pears. Plunge into cold water or hold under the tap for a few seconds, then pack into proper bottling jars.

Filling-up must be done with a solution of salt, lemon-juice and *boiled water* that has become cold. The proportion is 2½ ozs. salt and 5 ozs. lemon-juice to every 4 quarts of water, these being added while the water is still hot and well stirred to dissolve the salt.

After the bottles have been filled with cold solution they are closed with rubbers, covers and rings or clips precisely as is done with fruit, and set on a false bottom in the pan, covered with cold water and gradually brought up to *boiling-point*. That is the main difference to be noted, namely, that vegetables require a higher temperature and a longer time than fruit for sterilisation.

An Important Point

As Vegetables have to be bottled at much greater heat than fruit it is necessary, when using Kilner jars which have screw-tops to loosen the pressure a little after screwing down, as the greater heat in the pan might cause a burst. Directly the bottles are lifted out of the pan, however, they must be screwed down as tightly as possible, and left so for at least a day.

Time of Boiling for Perfect Sterilisation

From the time the water in the pan reaches boiling-point it should be kept there for 1½ hours, and 2 hours will not be too long for peas. Indeed for peas and green beans it will be wise to boil for 2 hours first, then to remove and let the bottles stand over for three or four days, after this to stand in cold water again, bring up to boiling-point, and keep there for half an hour. After the second boiling test, see that the tops are sealed by the vacuum, remove all clips and rings and set the bottles away in the storeroom.

The first boiling destroys any germs that may be present when the vegetables are first treated ; the second destroys any that may have developed later, but it is only peas, beans and asparagus that are liable to germinate spores after a first sterilisation.

Peas, Beans and Carrots

For the country housewife the only vegetables that she will find it worth while to bottle are Green Peas, French Beans and Young Carrots. Of Asparagus it is not likely she will have enough to put away, but in case this does happen it is well to know that only the youngest tips are suitable, that the stalks should be cut the length of the bottle (up to the shoulder only) that the rough outer skin should be scraped off and that packing should be as tight as it is possible to make it. The asparagus should stand upright in boiling water for a few minutes before filling the bottles, then be rinsed in cold water. The bottles are filled up with salted water and lemon-juice precisely as is done with peas. Sterilise in water at boiling-point for $1\frac{1}{2}$ hours.

Young carrots only are worth bottling, and these should be of nice shape. They are scraped, or better still is it to let them stand a few minutes covered with hot water, and afterwards rub off the young skin with a cloth. Pack while warm, arranging tips up and down alternately so as to fill the space evenly. Some people like to pack carrots and peas in the same bottle, and they certainly look well. Sterilise for fully $1\frac{1}{2}$ hours. Green beans should be sterilised like peas, but if very young they can be done whole, if large slice as you would for ordinary cooking.

3. *Pickles, Chutneys and Ketchup*

HE things we find best worth preserving with vinegar are Shallots, Red Cabbage, Beetroot, Walnuts, Mushrooms, Red Plums, Peaches, Artichoke Bottoms, Gherkins and Damsons. Plums, Peaches and Damsons can be made into Sweet Pickle.

Sweet Pickles

For which Peaches have the skin rubbed off, while Plums and Damsons are pricked before treatment. The first-named are halved, stoned and loosely packed into jars which should be only three-parts filled, and plums also should not quite fill any jar or bottle used. The pickle mixture is made by boiling vinegar with sugar and spices such as stick cinnamon, allspice, a blade of mace and a few cloves. There should be an equal weight of sugar to vinegar, boiled together to obtain the full value of the spices. In the case of peaches and ripe plums it is sufficient to pour boiling liquid over the fruit and leave that to grow cold, then to seal and keep for a time before using. In the case of vegetables a little cooking in the boiling vinegar is desirable. All should be kept a few weeks before being used.

Vegetable Pickles

Cabbage should be finely shred with a sharp knife then laid on dishes or plates and liberally covered with salt, and so left for a couple of days. The salt then melts and forms a brine which should be drained off, when the cabbage can be packed into jars and the boiling vinegar with its spices and peppercorns poured over. The same process would apply to shallots, cauliflower, beetroot, etc., namely, that of salting first, then pouring the hot vinegar and spices over and sealing down before cooling takes place.

Young gherkins and cucumbers are steeped in salt and water then brought up to boiling-point and set away to cool. After packing them in jars pour boiling vinegar over, using a few peppercorns to flavour. Some red peppers or capsicums improve both flavour and appearance of gherkins.

Shallots require plenty of peppers adding to the vinegar, but it is better to strain this before pouring over the onions which, in their turn, have been boiled in salt and water a few minutes, then drained and put under the water tap a moment or two. This keeps them more delicate in appearance and the full flavour of the onion is retained.

Green Walnuts are picked before the shell has begun to form, and they, too, are pricked all over with a darning-needle before being put into a strong brine. After three days take them out, lay on sheets in the sun, turning frequently, until they have become black all over. Then pack into jars and pour boiling spiced vinegar over. Pick early in July, or as soon as of fair size.

Pickled Mushrooms want careful peeling and to be lightly dropped into glass jars, being filled up with strong salted water just off the boil first, left to cool, this poured off and spiced vinegar just off the boil put in. Cork or seal immediately, then put away for at least a fortnight before using. Only button mushrooms should be pickled, not the larger kind.

Pickled Nasturtium Seeds are very useful for taking the place of Capers in sauces, and they should be picked while green, dropping them into a wide-mouthed bottle, which when full can have boiling vinegar flavoured with salt and peppercorns poured over, through a strainer. Cork immediately and keep at least a month.

To Seal Pickles

If using bottles, those of the ordinary wide-mouthed type without caps, a good cork and some sealing-wax give security ; small metal caps are to be bought that will fit over many types of sauce-bottle ; or if using the same kind of jar as one would for fruit—and this is certainly the best for Sweet Pickles, one would use rubber ring, cap and clip also, but it is not so essential to form a vacuum, although if boiling vinegar has been poured in and the ring and cap are put on immediately, a vacuum will often form of its own accord.

To Make Chutney

In this type of Sweet Pickle there is opportunity for making experiment and for using fancy and ingenuity. Many people have favourite recipes of their own for which they claim a preference above all others, but in the main the ingredients are similar in one and all.

Acid fruits such as gooseberries, apples, plums tomatoes, are the base, and hot spices like ginger and peppers are needed, while sugar, raisins, dates, garlic and shallots, cucumbers and green peppers are all wanted or can be used in different combinations.

The difference between a chutney and a pickle is that the first-named resembles a paste, is nearly always sweet, and very fruity. In making chutney use an enamelled pan (or aluminium) but not a brass or copper one. A chutney should be smooth and rich, not sharp or acrid like a pickle.

In bottling chutney use wide-mouthed bottles and line the corks by placing parchment or greaseproof paper over them, and over the cork run melted sealing-wax. Or preference may be given to small jam-jars of glass that can be tied down with bladder or wax paper. It will keep perfectly well either way. If, however, metal-capped jars are used, insert a round of waxed paper between as the acid contents must not touch metal.

SOME CHUTNEY SUGGESTIONS

(1) Apples, Onions, Stoned Raisins, Ginger, Brown Sugar, Mustard-seed, Cayenne, Allspice and Brown Vinegar with a little Salt, combined together are excellent. The sugar should be half the weight of the apples, the onions one-third, the raisins a quarter, and the spices and other things are according to discretion and taste. Cook all together in the pan until reduced to a pulp. It should be thick and brown.

(2) Green Gooseberries, Stoned Raisins, Onion, crushed Mustard-seed, Mixed Spice, Sugar and Vinegar with a little Salt, make another combination which also should simmer until it is of a rich thick consistency.

(3) Stoned Plums, Minced Onions, Raisins, Brown Sugar, one or two Apples, some Chopped Chillies, Allspice, Brown Vinegar, a little Salt, Cloves and Nutmeg, make another combination.

(4) Green or Ripe Tomatoes, with some Apples, Chopped Onions, Stoned Raisins, Moist Sugar, Ginger, Allspice, Cinnamon, Vinegar, Cloves and Peppercorns, and a little Salt, make excellent Chutney, the tomatoes being peeled and sliced, the apples ditto before adding the other things. Cook to a rich consistency.

(5) Marrow and Apples, Shallots, Sugar, Bruised Ginger, Grated Rind and Juice of one or two Lemons, with Vinegar just to cover all, then cooked to a smooth consistency but not allowed to become too dark, makes another very pleasant chutney.

(6) Stoned Dates, Stoned Raisins, Chopped Shallots, Red Chillies, Vinegar and Sugar, with a little Salt, and all cooked until very soft and tender, makes yet another nice combination.

MINT VINEGAR

The Mint must be gathered young and fresh. Pick the leaves from the stalks and fill a bottle with them. Cover with cold vinegar, let them infuse four or five days, then strain into a saucepan, add some lumps of sugar, heat but do not boil, and when cool pour into a fresh bottle and cork well.

MINT JELLY

Chop some young fresh mint ; dissolve in some sweet wine vinegar a packet of lemon jelly crystals, add enough water to make half-pint and add a little white sugar. Mix the fresh mint with the dissolved crystals, and pour into small glass jars.

Or use the juice of green apples, boiled and strained and sweetened as for jelly, adding freshly-chopped mint before putting into jars.

SOME KETCHUPS

Ketchups are strong flavours used in sauces and gravies, but are not for table use as condiments. They make a great difference to the savouriness of made-over dishes and sauces, and can so often be made from trimmings, as from the peelings of mushrooms, that they should find a place in the housewife's cupboard.

MUSHROOM KETCHUP

Pick large black mushrooms, and use the peelings of others, but see that all are perfectly dry and free from grit. Place in a large jar and cover with a layer of salt and leave for three days, stirring occasionally. At the end of that time set the pan on the stove and heat slowly until juice flows freely, then strain the mushrooms through a cloth and press but do not squeeze it.

Put the liquor obtained into a saucepan and add a little allspice, a little ground ginger, a dash of cayenne, bring almost to boiling-point, then strain again before pouring into a bottle and corking it.

WALNUT KETCHUP

Use green walnuts which should be very young and tender ; bruise slightly and put into a jar with a handful of salt and sufficient vinegar just to cover them. Let them remain for a week, stirring now and then. Drain off the liquor into a saucepan and add to it a handful of chopped shallots, a piece of horseradish roughly grated, a piece of stem ginger, some peppercorns, a grated nutmeg, and some cloves. Simmer all for half an hour, then strain clear and bottle, covering the cork with wax.

ELDERBERRY KETCHUP

Pick a quart of ripe elderberries, place in a stone jar and cover with vinegar, cook in slow oven for three hours, then strain, and to the liquor add some shallots, a blade of mace, a few cloves, ½ lb. sugar and a few peppers. Simmer gently for an hour then strain and bottle well.

TOMATO KETCHUP

Take ripe tomatoes, say 2 lbs., 2 pepper-pods, 2 onions, 2 tablespoonfuls of salt, 4 of brown sugar, a mixed spoonful of ground ginger, mustard, nutmeg and spice, and a quart of vinegar.

Peel and crush the tomatoes, peel and chop apples, mince the onions and mix with other ingredients. Cook all together for nearly two hours. Rub through a coarse sieve, bottle whilst hot and seal well, keep in cool place.

4. *Recipes for combining Vegetables, Cheese and Pastes*

Contributed by a Connoisseur

EVERY man claims to be a Connoisseur in the matter of Vegetable cookery, and the following Recipes have been contributed by a critic fully entitled to make the claim, although he has, in certain instances, left them, literally to be taken with a grain of salt !

MACEDOINE OF VEGETABLES

Take equal quantities, by measure, of fresh peas, small French beans (or cut into inch lengths), sliced young carrots and turnips. Simmer in a little water. When cooked, but still whole, drain and scatter them in a pan containing a strong stock of rice or Jerusalem artichokes. Use only enough stock to form a liberal binding. When well mixed, turn in a plain mould to set. Serve with a salad dressing or a piquante sauce.

VEGETABLE PIE

Soak a breakfastcupful of butter beans or haricots for at least 12 hours. Wash and place in a pan with water, barely enough to cover them ; simmer till tender. Clean about the same quantity of Jerusalem artichokes, slice and simmer in salted water, just sufficient to cover them. Fry two good-sized onions in fat. When browned, add to them three large carrots in thin slices, stir well and add a few drops of water, only enough to prevent burning. Flavour with salt and pepper. Stew slowly until soft. Meanwhile boil in their jackets a pound of potatoes. When cooked, remove skins and mash, mixing in a little milk or water, a pinch of salt and a nut of butter. (Better results will be obtained if two tablespoonfuls of flour are worked into the potato paste.) Now turn the Jerusalem artichokes and beans on to the onions and carrots and stir up with them two beaten eggs or an equivalent amount of prepared dried egg powder. Line a buttered pie-dish with about half the mashed potatoes. Pour in the hot mixture and cover with the remainder of the potato, making a hole at the top for the escape of steam. Place in a quick oven until a nice brown. The pie can be eaten hot or cold, and will warm up well.

It is very savoury ; most people have difficulty in believing that it contains no meat.

While the above mixture of vegetables is a good one, almost any others can be used, even green stuff. But the fried onion must not be omitted, and it should be remembered that much of the richness is due to the carrots and to the artichokes.

Peas or broad beans make good substitutes for the haricots.

Cheese Cauliflower

Place the cauliflower to boil in salted water. Take equal parts of breadcrumbs and grated cheese, adding enough water from the pot to form a thin paste. Work quite smooth. Strain the cauliflower, place in a baking dish, cover with the sauce and place in the oven to give the whole a light golden hue.

Stuffed Cabbage

Take a large, firm cabbage. Remove outer loose

leaves. Dip into boiling water for ten minutes. Drain, cut into halves and remove the heart. Hash the heart and mix with a little breadcrumb or oatmeal, minced onion, minced meat (preferably cold boiled pork, ham or bacon), and add a little cabbage water with a beaten-up egg. Stuff the two hollow halves, place together, tie up and place in a net. Simmer in stock until thoroughly cooked.

MARROW FLOWERS STUFFED

In Provence the over-abundance of flowers of the *courge* (vegetable marrow) plants—those which are slow in forming fruit or are best removed to assist the plant, are plucked off, wiped and placed bell downwards on a plate. Then a forcemeat is prepared of parboiled rice, herbs and eggs, with which the flowers are stuffed. Next they are tied with thread and gently stewed in vegetable stock (the rice water flavoured with onion, parsley or any other vegetable). The stuffed flowers are placed round a meat dish or served as an *entremet*.

Forcemeat.—For the stuffing boil a cupful of rice in a little water, add three chopped button onions, a spoonful of chopped parsley, and any other herb. When nearly cooked strain, add a beaten egg and a nut of butter. Flavour with pepper and salt.

STUFFED PEPPERS

The large green pods of the pepper plant (capsicum) are cut open and the seeds removed. These seeds are hashed up with breadcrumb, finely chopped onion and parsley ; the whole is moistened with vegetable stock and a beaten-up egg and flavoured with pepper and salt and used as a stuffing for the pods, which are then stewed in a little meat or vegetable stock. If desired, remnants of meat can be minced and added to the stuffing.

STUFFED TOMATOES

Take half a dozen ripe, but not over-ripe, tomatoes. Cut in halves and remove the seeds. Prepare a forcemeat of a breakfastcupful of breadcrumbs and one tablespoonful each of grated cheese, chopped onions and kitchen herbs (parsley, with basil or lemon thyme) ; moisten with one egg. Stuff the tomatoes ; breadcrumb them and crown each with a nut of butter, or a few drops of olive oil. Fry or place in a baking dish in a quick oven.

STUFFED ONIONS

Parboil 6 large onions. Cut in halves, crossways, and remove the inner rings, and use these chopped, to form the forcemeat, as for the tomatoes. Stuff the onions and fry or bake.

STUFFED VEGETABLE MARROW

Parboil a vegetable marrow after it has been peeled, cut in halves and seeded. Drain and stuff with the same forcemeat as for tomatoes, and bake.

Or, prepare forcemeat with a cupful of parboiled rice, half a cupful of minced veal or mutton, a tablespoonful each of minced onions and parsley with basil or lemon thyme. Stuff the vegetable with this and stew gently in stock.

FRENCH EGGS

Steam 6 potatoes and boil 3 eggs. Place the potatoes·in a pan, cut the eggs in quarters, place over the potatoes ; breadcrumb and sprinkle with shaved butter or fat. Place in the oven and bake.

PROVENCAL POTATOES

Boil a pound of small round or kidney new potatoes in their jackets, together with half the number of button onions. Drain. Peel the potatoes and toss them with the onions in butter, adding a little salt and chopped parsley.

PROVENCAL PEAS

Place a pound of fresh peas in just enough water to cover them, together with half a dozen button onions, flavouring with salt. When cooked they should be nearly dry. Add two ounces of butter, toss well and serve hot.

STEWED CUCUMBER

Peel a large cucumber, removing both ends, which are apt to be bitter. Cut into slices about two inches thick and stew slowly in a mixture of milk and water or in stock, but use only enough liquor to form a sauce. Flavour with salt and pepper. Both dressings are good ; the prettiest effect is obtained with the transparent slices in the white sauce.

CURRIED LENTILS

Steep a breakfastcupful of lentils (the grey are the best) in water for about 12 hours. Boil in just enough water to cover them until tender. Cut up a large onion in shreds and fry until dark brown. Mix in a teacupful of water two teaspoonfuls of curry powder. Add to the frying onions and allow to boil for five minutes, stirring well. Then mix in the lentils. Serve alone or with a little plain boiled rice or mashed potatoes. The flavour is improved if grated lemon peel (about a teaspoonful) or the juice of a lemon is added.

Stewed Lettuce

Cos lettuce when a little too coarse for saladings, or beginning to run to seed, is excellent stewed, either in a half and half mixture of milk and water, flavoured with salt and pepper, or in meat or vegetable stock thickened with a little arrowroot or cornflour. Only use enough liquor to form a sauce.

Spinach Beet Purée

Spinach beet leaves are treated like ordinary spinach, but if the ribs are thick, cut them out. Wash the leaves and simmer in a very little water, with some salt. When quite tender, drain, hash as small as possible ; return to the pan, add butter and stir to form a smooth paste. Serve with fried sippets as a plain vegetable, as a surround for boiled or roast meat, or as a bed for poached or scrambled eggs.

Spinach Beet Fritters

The stems and the ribs of the spinach beet should be boiled in salted water for five minutes, then dipped in a thin batter and fried.

Or the stems can be treated like Sea Kale or Asparagus and served either hot or cold with suitable sauces.

Spinach Beet Cakes

Parboil six large leaves of spinach beet. Remove the stems and thick ribs, which cut into small pieces. Hash the leaf parts. Add these, together with six coarsely hashed pickled olives in a batter, made with two ounces of flour or potato meal mixed into a smooth paste with a little water in which the spinach was cooked. Beat up an egg and mix with salt and pepper to taste. Fry the mixtures either like a thick pancake or as fritters.

In Provence the above mixtures, with a tablespoonful of oil and an extra egg, are placed in shallow cases of short or puff paste. Ripe salted olives (brown and full of oil) are sprinkled over the top and the whole baked. It is a somewhat rich preparation.

POTATO TOAST

Steam some potatoes in their jackets, peel, mash, adding an ounce of flour and an ounce of fat to every pound of potato and milk or water as necessary. Flavour with salt and a dash of pepper. Roll out into a flat cake about two inches thick. Place on a baking tin and put into a quick oven until a rich yellow brown.

Such toasts may form the foundation of poached eggs, vegetable *purées*, melted cheese, hashes or other mixtures.

If a little sugar, syrup or honey is substituted for the salt and pepper the toasts will make good foundations for a variety of sweet dishes.

MAIZE FLOUR TOAST

Sift a cupful of yellow maize meal in a quart of water. Bring to the boil, stirring well and adding a little salt and an ounce of fat. When thoroughly cooked (after 30 minutes' boiling) pour into a shallow dish to set. It should not be much more than an inch thick. When cold place on a baking tin and bake until nicely brown.

This can be used instead of the potato toast, and as with the above a sweet variety can be prepared.

CHEESE SPONGE

Take two parts of breadcrumbs parched in a slow oven, two parts of grated or broken cheese and one part of fat. Melt the fat in a little milk or beer, stir in the cheese and then the breadcrumbs, beating into a froth with a fork. Pour the sponge over toast, a steamed cauliflower or braised seakale. (Cheese treated in this way is thoroughly digestible.)

POLENTA CHEESE

Prepare a porridge of yellow maize meal by sifting a breakfastcupful of meal in a pint and a half of boiling water, adding a pinch of salt and an ounce of butter. Stir to keep smooth, keeping over the fire for at least 30 minutes. Pour into a dish to set. Then cut in horizontal slices 2 inches thick, place these in a buttered pie-dish with a layer of grated cheese between the slices. Butter the top and bake. Serve with a sauce of thickened meat stock or tomato sauce.

RISSOTTO

Sprinkle a breakfastcupful of rice in a pint of boiling stock or plain salted water. Fry a large sliced onion in two ounces of fat. Season with salt. Pour the rice over the onion, stir well until cooked and then bind with an egg, well beaten up. If liked, two ounces of grated cheese may be added. To use up small remnants of meat, mince and stir into the rice. The egg can be omitted.

SCRAMBLED EGGS AND TOMATOES

Beat up three eggs, or the equivalent amount of egg

powder. Poach three large tomatoes in boiling water and skin them. Fry a small onion, sliced, in half an ounce of fat and add to it the skinned tomatoes, cut small and seasoned with pepper and salt. Place on fire to simmer slowly until soft. Then put half an ounce of fat in a pan, add the eggs, beat up into a froth and mix in the tomatoes, stirring vigorously. Pour over hot potato or maize toast, and serve at once.

SCRAMBLED EGGS AND JERUSALEM ARTICHOKES

Proceed as above, boiling the artichokes in a very little water and working them into a smooth paste.

Mushrooms, asparagus tops, spinach or sorrel may be treated in the same way.

MELTED CHEESE AND MAIZE TOAST

For this purpose any kind of cheese can be used, even if stale, and the very rind (scraped clean) can be grated with the rest. In preparing the toast (see above) add two ounces of grated cheese to the porridge.

Take four eggs, or the equivalent of egg powder, and pour into a pan containing an ounce of melted fat. Beat up well and add gradually four ounces of cheese, a pinch of salt and a little pepper. When nice and frothy, pour over the hot toast and place in the oven for a few minutes.

Serve with mustard, using tarragon vinegar instead of water.

POTATO CRUST FOR PIES AND TARTS

Steam the potatoes in their jackets. When cooked, peel and mash. For every pound of potatoes add two ounces of flour (sifted in gradually), two ounces of fat, an ounce of sugar (or two of syrup), two eggs or their equivalent in powder and sufficient milk or water to form a thick paste. If water is used slightly increase the allowance of fat. This paste can be rolled out once and then placed in a buttered dish to receive any fruit or pudding mixture desired. If a pie, put on the top crust rather thick and leave a big hole in the middle for the escape of steam.

A savoury crust can be prepared in the same way, omitting the sugar and substituting a little salt.

Rice Fritters Sweetened

Boil some rice in sweetened milk. Flavour with vanilla, almond or with the juice of a lemon. Allow to cool. Form into balls or flat cakes and fry a golden colour in a deep bath of dripping. Serve hot.

MILK AND EGGS

IV

1. *How to deal with a Glut*

MILK is a commodity that cannot be counted upon to remain regular in amount except it is obtained at second-hand through a trader who undertakes to deliver a precise quantity day by day. Where country people keep one or more cows of their own there will be uncertainty as to yield at different seasons, and there will be times when a sudden plenty presents a more difficult problem than scarcity ever can do. Where pigs and chickens are kept it is not unlikely that any overplus will find its way to them, but sometimes there are better ways of disposing of it and it is just as well to be provided with plans.

Where milk is to be had in great plenty, and there is no dairy and no butter-making apparatus available, the housewife bethinks herself of getting all the cream she can and of making sweet and savoury dishes and small cheeses that will keep for a time ; she may make bread and quick scones with what has already become slightly soured, and she may use the residue for washing paint and linoleum ! But there is a more varied list of possible uses open to those who have one or two cows of their own and who will, at times, have liberal supplies which they want to put to profitable use.

CLOTTED CREAM

First thoughts turn to the enjoyment of an abundance

of rich cream for the table and of means of keeping this sweet.

In making Clotted Cream it is necessary to use rich milk, and that is why the best cream is produced from districts where special breeds of cows feed on rich pasturage, but in most districts there is a period when the milk produced is much richer in fat than at other times, and that is the moment to choose for experimenting with it.

Clotted cream is made by taking whole milk, warm from the cow and straining it carefully into shallow pans. The pans should not be more than 7 inches deep and should be wide across the top ; they are best if made of bright aluminium. Set in a cool place, the pans should be left undisturbed for some twelve hours.

After twelve hours or rather longer, the pans should be carried very carefully by two people and placed on the top of a stove or, better still, over a large boiling-pan containing boiling water, so that steam can play upon their contents. The cream should reach a temperature of 180 degrees in about half an hour, after which the pans should be removed to cool off gradually. Heating should never be done too quickly or the cream will be greasy, and while heating over water is preferred it is quite often done over the ordinary kitchen range.

When the pans have cooled to their original temperature the cream can be taken off in the thick, clotted condition that is usually seen and it is better to do this on a sieve over which a piece of muslin has been laid as there may be some need to drain it ; but if for immediate use, it can be skimmed into dishes straight away. One pound's weight of rich cream should be obtained from a gallon and a half of Jersey milk, but rather more is needed to produce the same from ordinary Shorthorns.

CREAM CHEESE

Small soft cheeses are extensively made during the summer months where milk is plentiful, and their flavour and type will vary in almost every district. The better the cream the better the cheese, yet many people think that almost any milk or cream will do for cheese-making. It must, at least, be perfectly sweet and fresh if the cheese is to be satisfactory. The old method of draining the cream by hanging-up in a bag of muslin or cheesecloth and letting it remain some days is a mistake, as very often by the time the contents have stopped draining the cream will have acquired a bad flavour.

TYPES OF CREAM CHEESE

Usually there are two types of cream cheese, one obtained from double-thick cream, the other from thin cream thickened with rennet before draining. A sweet cream cheese is obtained from cream that has been standing twelve hours, but if wanting to make it more quickly a small quantity of " starter " is put in as soon as new cream has cooled down to 70 degrees. This starter may be a culture generally used by cheese-makers, or a little clean soured milk.

" DOUBLE-CREAM " CHEESE

A reliable method of making this is the following : Take off the thickest cream into a clean can and stand this in a pail of cold water for several hours, then drain it in or over fine longcloth spread over a wooden bowl or board. Use another board to press out superfluous moisture when drainage has taken place. Drainage and pressure should be gentle at first otherwise the pores of the cloth get filled with cream. The cloth should be opened out once or twice and scraped during the first hour, after which the top board should be weighted. If the cream was thick and was well cooled before draining it should be ready to mould in three or four hours' time after weighting. Small moulds are used lined with strips of muslin or parchment paper for cheese that are intended for sale, and a wooden palette-knife is used for filling these ; but for household use they would not be necessary as the cheese can be served on clean green leaves or in fancy dishes.

" Single-Cream " Cheese

Very good cheeses from cream of a poorer quality can be made by adding three or four drops of rennet to a pint of cream containing perhaps only 25 to 30 per cent of fat. This should be put in immediately after the cream has been cooled down to 70 degrees. It is skimmed up with a ladle, pressed for draining, and formed into shapes.

Milk Cheese with a very small proportion of cream is made by mixing whole milk with some drained cream and a little rennet.

Home-made Butter

Country people who keep one or more cows ought to be able to make their own butter, even although the yield of milk may vary a good deal both in quantity and quality. If there is even a moderate supply of milk it is well worth while obtaining a separator as where that is used the yield of fat will be from 90 to 92 per cent as against 80 per cent by skimming   A word of warning in regard to the placing of the separator may not be out of place. Any vibration or unsteadiness will prevent the proper working of the machine, therefore see that the floor is perfectly level and that all the parts are firmly fixed and kept oiled, so that action may be steady and regular.

" Ripened " cream, that is, cream one or two days old, will yield more butter than cream that is freshly obtained, but it is, of course, understood that it does not wait until it begins to turn ; three days may be allowed in winter weather, but not more than two in summertime, even in the coolest keeping-place.

Butter-making

Sometimes there is difficulty in getting the butter to " come ", even after all precautions have been taken in regard to the cream and the churn and the weather. Difficulties in churning may be experienced in all weathers, but are most likely to occur in the winter months. The cream will be " sleepy " and the butter will refuse to form, or will cling to the churn instead of dropping as the churn revolves. Many reasons may account for this. The churn may be over-full, or the cream at too high or too low a temperature, be too thick or have been kept too long. There may have been failure to ventilate the churn, or soap may have been used in cleaning it . . . any of these faults will account for a failure to produce butter or for what is called " sleepiness " in cream.

The churn should never be more than half-full at any time, and when " sleepiness " occurs make a pause at the end of each revolution and reverse the turning. Do this several times.

Churning

Scald the churn first, then cool with spring water, and pour in the cream skimmed from milk that has been standing at least 24 hours—this may have been taken at two skimmings.

Churn rather fast, until butter-flakes forming on the top and sides of the churn show that the desired end is near, then churn more slowly, but always with a regular motion. Should the butter come slowly, in warm weather, pour a little cold water into the churn. Take up with the perforated dasher, have ready some clean and very cold water in a wooden bowl and plunge the dasher into this. The butter flakes should float off leaving the dasher free. Having collected every particle of butter, squeeze and press this between flat butter hands to strain off all buttermilk, then set in a cool place to harden a little before further squeezing and moulding the butter into shape. This is the time to add salt, in the proportion of a dessertspoonful to every pound. The last working-up is the time when dexterity and skill show themselves ; shape and mark as taste dictates, but when moulded wrap in wet muslin that has not been touched with soap or starch. If for keeping a long time press down into stone jars that are perfectly clean and sprinkle salt over the top, or put a piece of muslin over the butter first and then a thick layer of salt. Keep in a very cool place.

WRONG FLAVOURS IN BUTTER

These may be due to several causes, i.e., to faulty methods in the cowshed, where the milk gets contaminated, or to faulty ripening of the cream, or to bad management in the feeding of the cows, especially if certain foods are given in excess, turnips providing a particularly common example. Where cows must be fed on certain foods, tainting can be partially avoided by feeding them after instead of before milking.

Colour in butter is influenced by the breed as well as by the feeding of the cows ; the Channel Islands breed always produces the most highly-coloured butter, but with any breed the colour as well as the flavour of the butter is improved when the cows are out to grass.

JUNKETS

Use fresh new milk that has neither been separated nor skimmed, if rich junkets are desired, and allow a teaspoonful of junket-powder to a pint of milk. It is not usual to sweeten new milk used for junket as sugar and cream are eaten with it, but before bringing to table grate a little nutmeg over the top.

CURDS AND WHEY

New milk, from which no cream has been taken, makes the best curd and a little rennet, a very little, is used to produce the curd which should be taken up in a sieve and drained over a bowl. What comes out by draining is the whey, and this, when cold, is a most refreshing and wholesome drink. Sometimes curds and whey together are served in saucers with fresh cream and sugar on top. All methods of serving curds and cream make this an acceptable dessert, but in addition the curd is often pressed into a mould to exclude all whey and this solid curd is sold by weight for eating with cooked fruit.

CHEESE-CAKES FROM CURDS

Solid Curd is often used for making a filling for pastry cases, and when so used is mixed with sugar, salt, spice, one or more beaten eggs, and possibly a few washed currants. A little milk added prevents it from setting too stiff after baking. A border of pastry round a fancy dish, or a lining of paste in a pie-dish, the curd mixture poured in and the whole baked until lightly browned on top makes a simple and wholesome pudding.

Buttermilk for Scones

Uses for buttermilk—the milk left after butter has been taken from the churn, are many, since that is deemed an excellent feeding-stuff for pigs and poultry, and equally good for humankind.

For making cakes and scones buttermilk is ideal, being far lighter than fresh milk, with a natural effervescent quality that aerates the mixture, especially when used in conjunction with a small amount of carbonate of soda.

Any type of scone can have buttermilk substituted for fresh milk in its recipe, but the lightest of all will be the perfectly plain tea-scone that has only flour, salt, a spoonful of soft butter, and sufficient buttermilk to make into a dough all worked together to a ball, then divided into small portions, flattened with the palm of the hand and baked on a girdle or in the oven. These will be all the lighter if a pinch of carbonate of soda is dissolved in the buttermilk just before using.

Skimmed Milk

Milk from which all the cream has been taken by a separator is sold at a cheaper price and is very useful for many cooking purposes, especially for making bread.

For bread it should not be watered down, but often is, while for cakes and puddings it is good enough when a little butter is added to return the fat that has been taken away. For rice puddings butter may not be necessary, but it improves the flavour and adds to the nourishment.

Poultry-breeders use skimmed milk mixed with rennet, left to become solid, as a food for chickens and especially as a food for turkeys when fattening them for market. For soup-making and indeed for mixing cakes and for most kitchen purposes skimmed milk is every whit as good as whole milk, as where extra enrichment is required cream is invariably added whether full milk has been used or not. This is worth remembering, because so often skimmed milk is treated with disfavour, especially in the country, and especially among the poor, to whom the difference in price would matter a great deal ! It is perfectly good milk, and the fat content can so easily be returned to it when necessary by adding a morsel of dripping, lard, butter or cream.

Skimmed milk is excellent for cleaning white enamelled furniture, paint, linoleum or oilcloth. If rubbed after washing, there is sufficient grease remaining to give a slight polish to the surface.

SKIMMED MILK AND BUTTERMILK FOR TOILET AND HOUSEHOLD USES

Country dwellers do not need to be reminded how useful milk can be in easing sunburn or for removing freckles, but the practice of bathing the face, hands and arms with milk will keep the skin soft and natural and prevent a good deal of the liability to scorching and chapping that is troublesome in hot weather where short sleeves and low-necked dresses are worn.

To bathe with milk after washing face and hands with warm soap and water is cooling, but the " tight " feeling that results after the milk has dried is not pleasant, therefore gentle rubbing is necessary until the milk has been absorbed by the skin. After that the feeling of coolness and softness left behind is its own reward. Some people use no soap at all in summertime where skimmed milk is plentiful, and providing they rub well with soft towels there will be no need, as milk is cleansing as well as feeding. A great deal depends on how much dust anyone is in contact with. After motoring, for instance, it is very necessary to wash the face with soap before rubbing in any emollient but for toilet use, morning and evening, milk may very well replace soap.

Skimmed milk will provide a sufficient stiffening to use for handkerchiefs and laces in place of starch, and is not sticky when used with a cool iron.

2. *Eggs : To Preserve for use in Winter*

HILE eggs are most plentiful in spring and the early summer months a country housekeeper will store as many as possible for use in winter, when they will be scarce. Various methods are favoured, but the one most generally adopted is the use of a solution of water-glass, although some still favour lime-water, and others rub over each egg with weak gum or with a greasy rag.

There are three varieties of water-glass to be bought in packets at any Stores, but all contain sodium silicate in differing proportions, requiring respectively 10, 15—20, or 25—27 times their bulk of clean boiling water to be used with them. The water and powder should be thoroughly stirred to ensure complete mixing and the solution should be quite cold before any eggs are put into it. If the solution evaporates by keeping, the quantity should be replenished as the eggs must be completely covered. Place a cover over the tub or pail in which the solution is kept to prevent evaporation and keep out dust. Galvanised iron bins or pails may be used. The eggs should remain in solution and taken out only as they are wanted for use. When taken out they will be sticky and should be washed and dried, but they will be found perfectly fresh, and at the end of six months or a year will taste and smell like fresh eggs. Before being put into the solution they should, however, be carefully inspected and tested in a strong light, and any rough or imperfect ones rejected.

IMPORTANT POINTS ABOUT PRESERVING EGGS

While eggs should be preserved or put into solution as soon as possible after they have been laid this should not be done until after they have cooled. An egg more than twenty-four hours old should not be preserved, nor should one that is dirty or defaced.

Eggs from hens fed upon grain and with plenty of liberty to run about are preferable for keeping purposes to those from hens kept in confinement. Infertile eggs keep longer than do those with the life-germ. In early spring eggs are " stronger " and will preserve better than those taken in summertime. Eggs should not be allowed to remain in a warm place either before or after preservation, and when stored they should be kept in a cool, well-ventilated cellar.

BROWN PICKLED EGGS

Cooked eggs in pickle are a very useful thing to have in reserve for making salads and attractive dishes.

Procure a number of fresh eggs and boil them for 15 minutes, then throw into cold water and when cooled strip off the shells. Meantime boil a quart of brown vinegar for ten minutes with ½ oz. of whole black peppers, ½ oz. Jamaica peppers, and the same quantity of stem-ginger and rough salt. Place the shelled eggs in a deep stone jar and pour the spiced vinegar over them while boiling-hot ; when cool, tie down with paper. Keep a month before using them. When cut open they look very pretty with their brown coating.

Milk and Eggs

Lemon Curd for Filling Cheesecakes

Ingredients :
 ½-lb. lump sugar ;
 ½-lb. fresh butter ;
 4 whole eggs ;
 Grated rind of 2 lemons, juice of 3.

Place butter, sugar and grated lemon-rind into an enamelled saucepan and cook gently for a minute or two, beat up the eggs and stir in, then add the strained juice.   Boil to a thick cream and pour into small jars which tie down for keeping.

Egg Emulsion (*For Sore Throats*)

Ingredients :
 Two eggs, perfectly new-laid, if possible warm
  from the nest.
 Juice of two ripe lemons.

Squeeze the juice of lemons over the eggs, keeping in a basin until shells have dissolved.   Beat up well with two large spoonfuls of thick honey and two of pure olive oil.   Continue beating until a perfectly smooth emulsion results, then bottle it and cork well. The dose is a tablespoonful.

Egg Nogg (*For Colds*)

Ingredients :
 Three eggs, whites and yolks beaten separately ;
 One pint full milk ;
 Half-teacup fine sugar ;
 Half-glassful best brandy ;
 Nutmeg to flavour.

Beat eggs, stir in the sugar, make milk very hot and add it gradually, lastly the brandy and nutmeg.   Drink as hot as possible.

EGG WINE

Boil together in a lined saucepan one or two glasses of white wine, with half the quantity of water ; sweeten to taste, and add a little nutmeg.   Beat well in a basin one or two eggs, with a spoonful of cold water to each egg ; pour the boiling wine very slowly into the basin, stirring steadily all the time, and then back into the saucepan.   Hold the saucepan with one hand over the fire for only a minute, and stir with the other.   Do not let the contents boil or they will be spoiled.

THE SPORTSMAN'S BAG

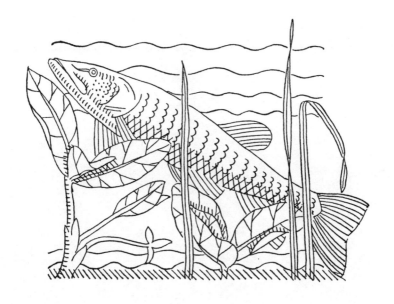

V

1. *Game*

A GOOD sportsman is said to deserve three things—a good gun, a good dog, and a good cook, and where birds and fish are concerned, it is probable that he will have no mean knowledge of how to treat these. If he is at hand he will be very willing to give his advice, but our concern is with the housewife who may have no one to guide her and who is anxious to do her best with what he offers from his bag.

HANGING GAME

It is part of every countrywoman's education that she should know what treatment to give to almost any type of country produce, irrespective of whether she gives it herself or directs others, and " treatment ", where Game and Fish are concerned, includes very much more than mere cooking. There is the matter of how long game should " hang ", for when birds have been shot with skill they will keep a considerable time, whereas others will have to be used at once. Hares and rabbits should have the paunch opened and emptied before they are hung, and some birds it will be necessary to draw before hanging up.

The birds most commonly received as presents are Grouse, Partridge and Pheasants, and occasionally a portion of Venison finds its way into the larder with Rabbits and Hares. Other wild birds come, too, but less often.

To Prepare Game-birds for Cooking

Plucking, drawing and trussing have to be done as with every other type of fowl, but the wing and tail feathers of pheasants should be carefully preserved, and in pulling off small feathers it is well to pull the opposite way from that in which they lie. Remove claws and heads, clean out the body and, if the bird has been kept a while, rinse the inside with vinegar and water, or dust with powdered charcoal. Truss like the ordinary fowl but wrap a piece of leaf fat over the breasts of partridge and pheasant, and tie small birds in the same. Roast in a quick oven, but avoid scorching.

Birds of doubtful age, whether wild or domestic fowl, are improved by Braising them in a Casserole, so that the flesh is kept moist, made tender, and the full savour kept in. Grouse, which are dry birds, are also much nicer if braised in a covered pot or tin. Wild-fowl, on the other hand, would be spoilt if treated so, as they require *quick* roasting and to be served *saignant*, that is, with the gravy running as soon as they are cut.

The Prairie-hen, Blackcock, Moorhen, Ptarmigan, and birds that have to work hard for their living are all suited to Braising, and as they are sometimes slightly bitter their flavour is improved by putting a little red wine into the pot. Most of the birds taken in sport are of a lean type, and need basting with butter while cooking, unless the casserole is used.

Grilling or Planking

It is the sportsman himself who is the best instructor when it is a question of cooking either birds or fish over an open fire or in front of it. The knack of building the fire and using the board and preparing the material can, however, be acquired, and once learnt is never forgotten. For Partridge, Woodcock, Pigeons, fresh Herring, Trout, and small river fish, this is an ideal method of cooking and is often the readiest one.

A word, however, about the Plank. This should be a strip of seasoned oakwood, about two inches thick, and should be kept rubbed with oil and a rag, and never washed but wrapped in paper. It is possible to use the plank under a gas griller, but then it is desirable to baste frequently and the light must be very low. Its real place is the open hearth.

Birds to be cooked by the Plank method must be cleaned after plucking and split down in half ; small fish are cleaned and split open, bigger fish are split down the back, and the most suitable portions of meat · to use are steaks and chops. Frequent turning and basting is needed.

A similar course is followed when using a Grill and this likewise should be cleaned by rubbing with fat or oil rather than by washing. A double grill is much handier than a single one that involves taking a fork to turn over what is being cooked.

COOKING WILDFOWL

The method of cooking the commoner kinds of wildfowl such as Wild Duck, Widgeon, Teal, Pochard and Shoveller, is simple roasting in the oven, and all of these must be served " piping hot ". In their case it is the accompaniments that require the attention of the cook rather than the birds themselves. Some good gravy with a little red wine in it is necessary, to which a few drops of acid lemon or vinegar give sharpness. The proper accompaniments are fruit salad made with sharp apples and oranges dressed with flavoured vinegar and oil, also chipped potatoes. Browned crumbs garnish wildfowl as well as pheasant, and red currant or rowan jelly is served with all.

GAME BIRDS

Quick roasting is best for all young and plump birds, and crisp fried crumbs, a boat of rich brown gravy, potato chips, and a suitable vegetable like celery or sea kale served under a creamy sauce are the correct accompaniments.

Birds that have to be cooked in portions, or those of a tougher type make excellent Game Pies and Puddings, as do mixed small birds of a miscellaneous order. These are often found in the bag during the shooting season and they are very useful as material for pies and pasties for the lunch basket. Used with a little beefsteak and a few mushrooms, plenty of seasoning, and a very good crust, they are most successful as pies, or for making a mould. The bones of game birds, excluding wildfowl which are apt to have a fishy flavour, are splendid for making stock.

JUGGED HARE

Cut up a hare into convenient pieces, wash well and dredge with flour. Take a pound of tender beefsteak with some fat to it and cut into pieces an inch square. A deep jar of glazed earthenware with close-fitting lid is the best to use and the portions of hare and steak are placed in this in alternate layers, mixing with them several small firm onions in each of which is a clove, and here and there a bit of mace.

Mix together a dessertspoonful of salt, a quarter-teaspoonful of ground black pepper, a pinch of cayenne, the grated rind of half a lemon, and tie together a bunch of savoury herbs ; spread these over the top and pour in sufficient water just to cover all. Close down and set the jar in a very moderate oven, or stand it in a deep pan with boiling water sufficient to come up to the neck of the jar but not over the top. Keep at simmering point at least five hours. Serve in a deep dish, using very little of the steak, but adding some forcemeat balls, and thickening the gravy if this seems necessary. Before serving add a glassful of wine, Burgundy or Claret, to the contents, and set a dish of red currant jelly on the table. Some add a portion of the blood of the hare to the gravy about ten minutes before dishing up, which makes it very dark in colour, but this addition is a matter for individual taste to determine.

Forcemeat Balls.—The forcemeat balls consist of minced ham, breadcrumbs, mixed herbs, seasoning, and an egg to bind, and should be first fried in hot fat to make them brown and crisp.

Salmi of Game Birds

This is a useful way of using a variety of small birds, and also a way of re-serving portions of cold hare, rabbit and game. It requires a rich gravy to be made first from the bones and carcasses, by long stewing, and this is strained, thickened and seasoned, and enriched with wine or sauce, then the trimmed portions of game or joints of birds are simmered in it. To make the gravy still richer fry several small onions, pare some mushrooms, tie together a bunch of sweet herbs, simmer all in butter or bacon dripping, then thicken with browned flour ; use bone stock and cook till of a good consistency, and strain before adding the portions of birds.

To Make a Terrine

This is a dish to be eaten cold and is useful for the sideboard. It is usually made in an oblong fireproof china dish or one of Pyrex glass, the meat being weighted after cooking so that a coating of jelly forms round it and any fat rises to the top. The meat of rabbits and hares, taken from the bones after stewing, and of game birds, is laid in the dish with strips of cooked ham or bacon between. A strong, well-seasoned and clear brown gravy is made from the bones and trimmings with some gelatine crystals added to it. Pour in as much of this gravy as the dish will hold, press down the meat to keep in place, and when cold the terrine should turn out in shape with jelly surrounding it, and be served cut in thin slices. If not required for eating at once the terrine can have a layer of melted fat poured on the top to exclude air and should be kept in a cold place. This kind of thing is an excellent standby in a country house as a sideboard dish or as something to take out for picnics.

When time cannot be given to making moulds with their appetising jellied coating, an easier method is to pot down all the meat from birds or rabbits that have been cooked in a casserole, with or without bacon and other additions, and from the bones and trimmings left after the best meat has been taken away, make soup or stock.

Potted meats, game and other, all need patience for pounding in a mortar to the right consistency, and careful judgment as to their seasoning and flavouring ; the labour of pounding is halved when the meats are put through a mincer first. Nothing is more useful to have in reserve than this kind of thing, as some will keep longer than others, especially in cold weather, if coated with melted suet and waxed paper. The secret of success in making potted meats is patience to obtain a smooth texture and then to flavour and season well.

GAME SOUP

This should be clear, of very good flavour, and stimulating. While strong, it should be free from any taint or tang such as would be given by birds that have become very " high ", therefore it is a mistake to think that what is not fit for roasting or stewing will do very well for making soup, but as long as they are sweet and fresh any bones, carcasses, pieces and portions, bits of brown skin, and trimmings will come in for soup-making. Put into a brown stone jar and cover with cold water, add some peeled onions, scraped carrots left whole, and a bunch of savoury herbs tied together ; add a few whole peppers and a spoonful of salt, also any strips of fried bacon-rind or bits of lean ham. A knuckle-bone of veal is a valuable addition if it can be got. Cook for hours, but very gently, letting the jar stand in the corner of the oven or at the back of a stove. Strain when cool and remove fat when cold. When re-heating this for serving up, add seasoning to taste if that seems necessary, also a little sherry. Serve quite clear but send round fried *crôutons* in a separate dish.

SAVOURY HERBS

The bunch of savoury herbs should consist of sprigs of parsley, thyme, chervil, tarragon, sweet basil and bay-leaf, marjoram and summer savoury, but not sage, as this last is apt to overpower the other flavours. Sage, however, is much in demand when geese and ducks, wild as well as tame, are being cooked, and for stuffings where these are made.

Devilled Game

This is a favourite dish with sportsmen and is generally eaten dry with a glass of wine. The portions of birds or joints should be only lightly cooked first, then should be scored rather deeply and rubbed or dusted with a powder made of salt, cayenne and curry-powder, a little mushroom powder if this is to be had, and a pinch of mustard. Broil the portions over a clear fire or toss in a frying-pan with a little butter ; serve brown, crisp and very hot, but not scorched or burnt. If sauce is wanted with devilled game it is made with a cup of rich brown stock, some mushroom ketchup, made mustard, the juice of a lemon and a little red wine. Moor game is particularly well suited to serving up in this way.

Quenelles of Game, Rabbit or Hare

Portions of cold cooked birds, etc., cut small and put through a mincer, with some peeled mushrooms also minced, can be mixed with a cupful of soaked breadcrumbs, seasoned well and made into small balls, then fried in boiling lard or bacon fat. If made no bigger than large marbles, fried crisp but not hard, they are delicious as an accompaniment to bacon for breakfast during the shooting season.

Venison

This is not very much appreciated by people unaccustomed to it, and yet as country folk are more likely to have it to deal with than are town dwellers, it cannot be omitted.   That it wants careful cooking, and treating with judgment and understanding is not to be denied, but once appreciated at its true value it is much liked.

Although roasting is not the only correct way of treating a cut taken from loin or haunch, it is the way we consider first.   If the venison has been hanging some time, as it should do before it is used, soak the outside by pouring lukewarm water over it in a bowl, then wipe dry and rub well with oil.   Next cover it with a thick paste made with flour and water and over this place sheets of buttered paper, and another thick sheet of plain paper last of all.   Set in a deep baking-tin with a little water at the bottom.   Put in a good hot oven, keeping the heat steady.   Pour a little more water into the tin now and then and baste the joint to keep the papers from shrivelling.   If the joint is a large one it will take from four to five hours to roast, if a small one about three hours will be enough, but care must be taken that the heat is not scorching it.

About half an hour before taking up remove the covering papers, also the paste, and probe with a skewer to see if the meat is tender.   Dredge dry flour over the top, and baste with hot fat, to give a nice brown crust or froth to the joint before dishing up.   Then it is ready to set on a hot dish.   A cut from the loin will provide a most acceptable roast.

As gravy, use stock made from trimmings and scraps of venison stewed in a pan, with water, peppercorns, blade of mace, salt and a pinch of cayenne.   Stew to reduce to half, strain and add three tablespoonfuls of red currant jelly, a wineglass of claret, and a little browned flour with butter.   Boil to make it smooth and slightly thick. Serve more currant jelly in a separate dish.

The neck and shoulder also provide roasting pieces, but by far the nicer way of using all but the best joints is to make a

VENISON PASTY

The name of this brings to mind the story of Friar Tuck and Sherwood Forest, and of how he feasted the disguised Richard Cœur-de-Lion upon this when that gallant gentleman shared the Friar's hospitality and found a safe hiding-place with him among the trees. Friar Tuck must have been a rare cook and have had resources of his own, one would think, but at any rate the recipe for Venison Pasty did not die with him if we are to believe old books.

It is said that he made strong gravy by stewing the portions he rejected as unfit for his pasty, while he cooked the better meat in another vessel. Meantime he made " a fair Paste " with flour and fat and salt well worked together and kneaded with water. With this he lined a dish keeping back enough to make a lid. Into this dish went the portions he had been cooking with special care, and doubtless with them he put some of the liquor from the other pan. Then one can imagine him laying on the lid of paste and making a hole in its middle with his not too small thumb. We are not told how he baked his pie, whether he had a brick oven or made one with hot stones, but he did bake it right well and when it was done he poured in more savoury liquor through that hole his thumb had made. Neither are we told whether like the modern cook he brushed his pie with egg to give it a fine glaze, but at least it was brown and crisp and full-flavoured, we are sure. And a hungry man like Richard would have no quarrel to find with it.

There are many in these modern days who would not give the time to making a Pasty so rich and good as that of Friar Tuck, yet have some need for a mode of using venison when it has come to them unexpectedly. For simple household requirements few things are better than

VENISON PUDDING

This can be rich yet is most wholesome.

It requires about 1½ lbs. of meat taken from any part providing it is well hung and freed from skin. To it should be added about half a pound of calf's liver, and the two meats should be cut into small portions of about an inch square, and rolled in seasoned flour, that is, flour mingled with salt, pepper, and grate of nutmeg.

A good suet crust made with ½ lb. finely shred fresh beef suet to 1 lb. flour and ½ oz. salt, mixed with cold water, is rolled out and used to line a greased basin, a portion reserved for the top. Fill lightly with pieces of venison and liver and then pour in enough good brown stock, seasoned and further enriched with a little red wine if that can be got then moisten the top crust and fasten down. Cover as usual with a cloth over greased paper and boil from four to five hours. It may require more stock to be thickened and flavoured and served hot in a separate sauce-tureen, but this pudding is rich yet wholesome, and is an acceptable change from beefsteak and kidney and other similar and more ordinary types.

Because venison requires such long cooking it is not so suitable for making a pie, but Rabbits, as everyone knows, are excellent for that purpose, and nothing is more welcome on a country table than a well-made

RABBIT PIE

It is made better still if a fairly generous amount of salt pork in strips is used with the lean rabbit meat. Skin, wash and cut the rabbit into joints, cutting the legs in half ; do not line the pie-dish with paste for this, but put a layer of salt pork in strips at the bottom, and another layer of the same over the rabbit. Flour each piece and sprinkle over all salt, pepper, grated lemon-rind and chopped parsley, then cover with warm water. Put a dish over this and simmer in the oven for an hour before putting on the crust—a good rich short crust, quite half an inch in thickness before baking, and well ornamented round the edges, then brushed over with egg and milk after it has been in the oven some twenty minutes, and allowed to bake another ten. This pie is nicest when served fresh and hot, with a vegetable accompaniment, say of Jerusalem artichokes in sauce, or cooked celery. Potatoes are superfluous where there is a pastry crust.

PIGEON PIE

Pluck, clean and wash two or more pigeons (quail or plovers could be used instead) and halve each, filling the cavities with a little forcemeat. Cook in a covered stewpan for a few minutes while preparing a rich crust. Line a buttered round tin with crust, lay in the birds and any spare forcemeat, put in as well a hard-boiled egg cut in slices, then put on a top crust leaving a hole in the middle for gravy to be poured in later. A little should be put in before the pie is baked but not enough to boil out or the appearance is spoilt. When the pie has reached a rich golden brown in an oven of moderate heat withdraw it and pour in more gravy, this having boiled in the meantime to reduce and make it strong. If doubtful of its setting to clear jelly add a little gelatine. The whole baking should take about an hour and a half.

Very small birds like woodcock and snipe are better roasted whole and served on toast. They are plucked and trussed but not always drawn, yet it is better they should be or there may be a bitter twang now and then. Little squares of pure leaf fat are usually bound over each breast. These birds are the " *bonnes-bouches* " of the sportsman, and cannot, like the partridge, be counted as a substantial contribution to a meal. But they are ideal for an invalid.

ACCOMPANIMENTS AND ACCESSORIES FOR GAME

The country housekeeper is sometimes at a loss to know what are the correct accompaniments to serve with game and fish with which she is unfamiliar, and if the sportsman himself is going to partake of them after she has cooked them she feels that her reputation will suffer if she fails in these details, however excellent in other respects her cooking may be. It is well known that the *chef* pays more attention to these details than to the main item when he has his way.

Accompaniments have to be studied carefully, for they may make or mar the whole dish, but also there are those other additional items that some people consider essential and others pass over as unimportant. In France, for instance, where wild geese are as freely eaten as tame birds, these would be considered as completely spoilt were they not served stuffed with a mash of sour russet apple, and if white wine were begrudged for their basting, or baked onions were not surrounding them. Our mode is to stuff geese with onion and serve apples as a sauce, and it is worth while to try both modes and endeavour to judge the difference between them.

Again, the heart of a green cabbage or of a lettuce is chosen to serve as a hiding-place for the body of a small bird such as a pigeon. The vegetable " case " is made pliable by first dipping into hot water and removing all outer leaves. After being cut open and laid flat the trussed bird is inserted, the leaves brought together again, set in a casserole with a cupful of stock poured over, and with lid on is stewed for perhaps an hour. The flavour is, of course, much improved if a few shallots and mushrooms are put with the stock. When the pigeon is lifted out of its hiding-place the stock is thickened and poured over it, onions, mushrooms and all.

Pigeons, plainly roasted, should " serve with " green peas and *sauté* new potatoes or chips, and butter, plenty of it, should be used for basting.

Peeled mushrooms, too, when cooked with butter, accord well with any small birds that are served on toast.

Cooked spinach is a suitable accompaniment to Plover and Quail, but is of too strong a flavour for Partridge ; with that we serve mild cabbage or cooked lettuces.

Chestnuts, roasted and peeled and covered with a creamy sauce accord remarkably well with roast Pheasant when that is accompanied by browned crumbs, bacon rolls and clear gravy, so, too, does Sea Kale, also Sprouts.

Braised Turnips suit Roast Hare, and Red Currant

Jelly is imperative. Fried and Chipped Potatoes, dry and crisp, are never out of place with any poultry or game birds. Good gravy, served alone, is welcomed with anything.

Grouse is a drier meat than most other birds and ought to have a liberal supply of butter for basting it while it is being cooked and must on no account be overcooked. Cold Grouse is a great delicacy, and so is Potted Grouse, especially if, again, plenty of butter is worked in with it.

GAME SOUPS

There is such a thing, too, as Grouse Soup, that is greatly fancied by people who like something out of the ordinary, and indeed any bones of game birds will make delicious stock if broken small and stewed gently for a long time. It is surprising how much savour and what an amount of gluten there is in bones of both poultry and game, therefore none should ever be thrown away until all their goodness has been extracted by long, gentle stewing. Very rich soup can be made from the stock with varying additions to give it distinctive character and some of the Italian pastes to give it substance.

2. *Freshwater Fish*

THIS has always to be used as quickly as possible after it has been caught, in fact, it is possibly never so good as when broiled over a coal-fire in the open by the the angler at the end of a day's sport. Yet very often it is sent on a long journey by rail or road, to be a puzzle and a perplexity to the one who receives it.

FRESH TROUT are never better than when they are served broiled over the coals or lightly fried after being dredged with dry flour. The fish should be split down the belly and cleaned, but the heads are not removed and they are not laid open for cooking, but done first on one side, then on the other. Even better is it to lay the fish in a shallow fireproof dish with butter in good supply, and bake them in a quick oven, sprigs of parsley with them and a sprinkle of salt and lemon-juice.

SALMON TROUT are, of course, quite another proposition, and should be treated in much the same way as large salmon, by boiling, steaming or baking in buttered paper, and should be served up with the same accompaniments of sauce, etc.

PERCH and other edible River Fish, which are somewhat lacking in distinctive flavour, are improved by being steeped in a marinade made with olive oil, vinegar, bay-leaves, pepper and salt, after they have been cleansed. When drained they can be dredged with flour and fried in very little fat and will be found quite pleasing.

A favourite method with French people is to cook river fish, of which they use many kinds, in what is called *Court-bouillon*, that is, reduced stock, made from a mixture of white wine, vinegar and water, with flavouring herbs such as parsley, thyme, bay-leaves cloves and shred onion, boiled together and strained, then used for covering the fish as it lies in a shallow dish, in which it simmers until done.

Another way of treating river fish such as Perch is to prepare a Water Souchy, using the smaller fish for this purpose after cleaning them, cutting them in pieces and boiling slowly with one or two roots of washed parsley, whole peppers and some salt. Strain this liquor through muslin and use it as a broth in which to lay the larger fish after cleaning these and cutting them across in deep gashes for crimping. A few minutes will suffice to cook the fish, and it can be served with pure butter melted and bunches of parsley that have been scalded in boiling water to brighten the colour. Cooked in this way any river fish will be firm even when quite tender, and will not fall away in bits as it is apt to do by any other mode.

The Pike is a winter fish, being at its best from September to March, and to be really likeable should not weigh much over three pounds, although many weigh much more. The roe should always be removed before cooking. It is more palatable when baked under paper and with herbs and onion than when boiled, but if boiled it should first have the head removed and be crimped. Sauces to serve with pike should be made piquant with shallots, vinegar, soy, etc., and the same sharp flavourings are necessary for Carp, which, being a pond fish, is apt to be unpalatable without them, although in certain country districts it is frequently eaten in the winter season. It is not good for food between May and November. It can be baked, steamed, boiled or fried, or used in a pie.

Sportsmen themselves prefer their freshwater fish to be grilled or roasted on a plank, and find them delicious cooked in this way, especially if done in the open air. For the home, they are better lightly floured and fried as before described, or laid in vinegar in a dish with black peppers and a little salt, and brought to boiling-point then set away to grow cold— precisely as one would treat Mackerel or Herrings when serving them " soused ".

PACKING FOR TRANSPORT

The only possible way of sending freshly-caught Trout or other river fish to friends is to wrap in layers of cut green grass and send in a straw carrier basket. It is the greatest mistake to use paper or pack in a box ; the air must get to the package, yet it must be handled as little as may be and should never be stuffed among a lot of other luggage. Baskets of the carrier shape can be hung in a railway van if this is requested by those who send them.

POTTED FISH

When a quantity of fish such as fresh herrings have to be used at once there is no better way than to cut off heads and tails, clean and cook with salt butter till tender, then pound in a bowl with pepper, salt and mace, and put down in pots with salt butter poured over.

Sardines and Pilchards, freshly caught, can be treated the same way, or they can be floured and tossed in a frying-basket in a pan of hot fat and served like Whitebait.

HERBS OF GRACE

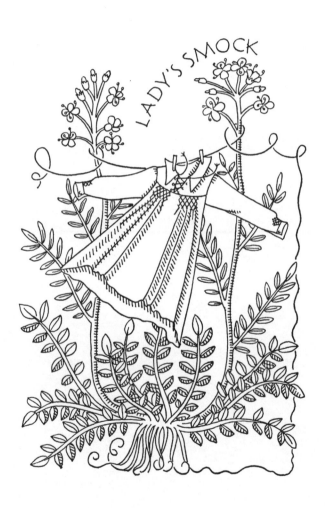

LADY'S SMOCK

VI

1. *Herbs : Useful and Fragrant*

THERE are Herbs of endless variety freely scattered throughout all countries, many of them known only to collectors and herbalists, and only a comparative few come into use among ordinary folk, and of these fewer still are met with in the average garden. Yet there is hardly anything that is so fascinating as a subject of study, and few things are more generally useful to a housewife.

Quite apart from their use in the kitchen, there is the Toilet-table, the Linen-chest and the Storeroom, and there is the fragrant bouquet for a friend or the packet of useful leaves for a brew, medical or simply soothing, as the case may be. Some women have so far extended their study and cultivation of herbs as to have made quite a profitable source of income from them, and this is by no means a difficult thing for any lover of a garden to do.

The country housewife, once started with a Herb-garden of her own will find a constant pleasure in discovering new plants to put into it ; she will not be content to show just what everyone else has, but will want the uncommon ones, the things that have secret charms and virtues. She will want to say with good old Sir Thomas More :

" There is manie a plant I entertayn in my

157

Garden and Paddock which the Fastidious would cast forthe. I like to teach my children the Uses of Common Things, to know, for instance, the Uses of the Flowers and Weeds that grow in our Fields and Hedges. Manie a poor Knave's Pottage would be improved were he but skilled in the properties of Burdock, of Purple Orchis, Lady's Smock and Brooklime and of Poor Man's Pepper. The rootes of Wild Succory and Water Arrowhead might agreablie change his Lenten diet and Glasswort afford him a Pickle for his mouthful of Salte Meat. Then there are the Cresses and Wood-sorrel for his Breakfast, and Salep for his hot evening Mess. For his Medicine there is Herb Twopence that will cure a hundred Ills, Camomile to soothe a raging Tooth, and the juice of Buttercup to clear his head by sneezing. Vervain cureth the ague and Crowfoot affords the least painfull of Blisters ; St. Anthony's Turnip is an Emetic ; Goosegrasse sweetens the Blood ; Woodruffe is good for the Liver ; Pimpernel promoteth Laughter and Poppy Sleep ; Thyme giveth pleasant Dreams and an Ashen branch driveth evil spirits from the Pillow. . . . As for Rosemarie, I let it run all over my garden walls not only because my bees love it, but because it is the Herb sacred to Remembrance and therefore to Friendship, whence a sprig of it hath a Dumb Language. . . ."

An old *Gardener's Guide*, printed as far back as 1842, advised :
        " Take a little strip for a herbiary ; let it be halfway betwixt the flower and the vegetable garden ; 'twill form a very appropriate transition stratum and

may be the means of being more under the eye of the mistress, and thus of recovering to our Soups and Salads some of the comparatively neglected Herbs such as Tarragon and French Sorrel, Purslane and Dill and Clary, and many more . . . this little Plot might be laid out in geometric pattern. . . ."

Geometric pattern or not, the Herb Plot set between the Kitchen and Flower Garden is a good idea, and yet one loves to see Lavender in generous clumps or making a hedge, Rosemary growing up against a garden wall, Southernwood in a border, the grey leaves of Sage contrasting with the green and purple of Thyme in fat bossy plants—and to have to look about for old favourites is a deal more interesting than to find them all ready to hand in geometric pattern ! Still, just how and where they are grown matters, after all, so very little compared with the value of having them in plenty and in as great variety as possible.

We no longer need to cut herbs and strew them to counteract unwholesome odours in dwelling-houses and public places, but we have gone to the other extreme and allowed their use as brews and teas to be superseded by drugs and patent medicines and flavouring essences. Even a country housewife has to plead guilty to this charge, although less addicted to purchasing cosmetics and lotions than a townswoman is.

Once a Herb-garden has been started, however, the fascination of it grows and grows ; from a few choice things for flavouring purposes one goes on to make discoveries concerning scented plants, to the collecting of leaves and flowers for drying, to their preserving in various ways, and uses for them as medicine increases as knowledge of their properties is gained. Always, we find, the beginning is made with Herbs grown for the Kitchen, so that is where we begin now.

PLANT KITCHEN HERBS TOGETHER

Whatever we may decide about the planting of fragrant plants and bushes, it is quite certain that it is an economy to plant the useful Kitchen Herbs in a bed of their own and close together. The bed can be bordered with parsley so that all the herbs wanted for an omelet or a " farce " can be picked at one stroke. Even so, it is astonishing to learn how many different plants will be grouped in that one bed . . . green and purple sage, the two thymes, the two savouries, basil, fennel, borage, chives, mint, lemon balm, sorrel, marjoram, rosemary, and even that list does not include them all !

FRAGRANT HERBS FOR THE GARDEN

Fragrant plants and shrubs that one would look for in a countrywoman's garden are so many that one finds it difficult to remember them all, but the commonest and the most useful include some that are forgotten in these modern days, so it is worth while to recall them. For instance, there is

Musk, Camomile, Broom, Tansy, Winter-sweet, Southernwood, Valerian, Verbena (the true Herb of Grace), Reseda or Mignonette, Daphne, Angelica, Almond, Agrimony, Pyrethrum (for powder), Lavender and Rosemary and Rue.

Most of these are easy to grow, and to them can be added several more when we are seeking fragrant plants for foliage to put with bulrushes and thistles or berries. Those going out of cultivation through neglect are Musk and Basil, two of the most precious we know.

Pot-herbs to Pick and Store

Taking the most commonly useful Kitchen Herbs first, which we hope to find together in their own little plot, let us see how to pick and ripen and store them to the best advantage, because they have their season and in the winter-time practically all of them, with the exception of the hardy Parsley, will have disappeared.

These herbs reach their strongest growth and have the maximum of scent and flavour when they flower—and even a green herb flowers, although in some cases the flower may be almost invisible. July and August are the months when Mint and Sage, Thyme and indeed most of the others named are in bloom, so that the stalks and branches should be cut then and dried by hanging them heads downward in the sun or in a cool greenhouse.

Drying Herbs for Colour

The slower method of natural drying tends to spoil the colour for sale purposes, and those who want to preserve this use stove-heat and dry quickly.

Parsley and Mint, for instance, which it is desired to keep a bright green, can be dried on sheets of paper in an oven with the door left open, and a few hours will suffice to make them ready to rub through a sieve. Another way to brighten the colour, especially with parsley, is to dip a bunch in very hot water for a second only, then to shake and dry it by the quick method ; mint also can be scalded in the same way. Sage is better dried naturally ; basil, fennel, borage and the savouries likewise ; colour is indifferent where they are concerned, but mint and parsley are often used for sprinkling over the surface of cooked dishes so a bright colour is desirable.

SIFT KITCHEN HERBS

After Drying all kitchen herbs should be rubbed through a wire sieve to sift the green leaf from bits of twig and stalk that it is most disagreeable to find in food. They should be dried until they will rub easily to a fine powder ; if limp this cannot be done.

STORE IN BOTTLES OR CASES

Most people put away their savoury herbs in stoppered bottles, but these are often awkward to handle when a cook is busy and has her hands in flour or perhaps a little greasy. An excellent method of storing kitchen herbs is to have hard paper cases with screwlids, such as can be bought for very little at Domestic Bazaars, and to use these for preference, as the lid is easily taken off and they are firm to handle, whereas nothing is more troublesome than a paper packet ! Bottles, of course, have the advantage of showing their contents well, and many people prefer them for this reason, but clear labelling should be adopted whatever method is used.

HERBS TO HANG IN BAGS

With things that it is not necessary to sift after drying and those one stores in bunches, like rosemary and camomile, broom and southernwood, it is enough to tie them up in paper bags, labelling each. Lavender is dried and rubbed down to separate it from leaves and twigs as only the dried flowers are wanted, but this is an easy matter. It should be ripe before being gathered and usually the months of July and August see this ready for reaping, although climate and situation decide the time in different districts,

OIL OF LAVENDER

Lavender is used for distilling, scent-making and for soap and other toilet purposes, when the essential oil is extracted from it by pressure. A great deal of the lavender grown in fields is used in this way. The housewife can, however, make her own lavender-water by infusing freshly-gathered pods in spirits of wine, and her own oil by pressing them between two slabs of marble or sheets of glass under heavy weight, and if anxious to do this she will not let the flowers become too dry. Most people, however, leave distillation and extraction to those whose business this is, and content themselves with drying and storing their own crop in sachets and bags.

DRIED LAVENDER

For use in the linen-chest and drawers, that is all that need be done to home-grown lavender, and there is even then quite a variety of pretty work to be done in winter evenings in the making of pillows, cushions, sachets and cases.

Rosemary and Verbena, also Mignonette, can be dried and used in sachets like lavender, or mixed together, but broom and tansy and valerian, have little scent when dried and need infusing to obtain their goodness from them ; angelica is candied, pyrethrum is dried and powdered, almond blossom is a flavouring for brandy like the aromatic bay laurel, although this last is often used dry and a leaf taken to flavour milk and custards. Musk has lost its scent and almost gone out of cultivation in recent years.

FRESH LEAVES FOR THE HOUSE

The scent of flowers is sometimes apt to be too

powerful in rooms, but that of leaves is never so, indeed the faint refreshing odour of leaves and wood is invigorating, and many people wisely gather young boughs in spring and keep them in jars for a long time in preference to having many cut flowers. In aromatic plants the scent goes right down into the wood, even to the roots, as one notices when among fruit bushes or fruit trees in blossom. Flowering trees that do not yield fruit like the White Willow are lovely for keeping in water as long as their bloom lasts, and Almond Blossom is another delightful thing for the same purpose.

Certain fragrant shrubs have a scent that is thought to be good as a preventive—the Sweet Bay Laurel has been considered a sure preventive of fevers, like the stronger-scented Feverfew, and there is good reason to believe that old traditions regarding the curative value of air coming off scented fields was founded on fact. It is a certainty that ozone is materially increased where the warmth of the sun draws out the scent of Lavender, Musk, Cherry, Clove, Fennel, Heliotrope and Eucalyptus. The not too-pleasant scent of Rue was for ages believed to be effective in warding off fevers. Certain it is that a few sprigs of Rue hung in a room will keep away flies from that apartment ! For long the Courts of Law used to be strewn with Rue, and so were the hustings at electioneering times. Tansy is another common herb that is also good for keeping flies out of a room, especially a sickroom.

Many vegetables and odorous plants belonging to the kitchen garden possess antiseptic qualities, and everyone knows that the ancient custom of strewing a floor with rushes and scented grass was not merely to give a pleasant odour, but quite as often to overcome unpleasant ones. It was at one time the custom to strew flowers and rushes in pews in churches, as Shakespeare has it :

" My lady's fair pew hath been strewn full with primroses, cowslips and violets, with mints and marigolds and marjoram."

People who despise the use of a scent-bottle will still agree that the increased cultivation and use of aromatic plants, somewhat after the old manner, but adapted to modern times, would be a gain to health, and certainly preferable to the lavish and increasing use of manufactured scents.

USES FOR FLOWERS AND LEAVES

The country housewife is most concerned with the uses she can make of scented leaves and flowers in her living-rooms and of how she may extract and preserve their antiseptic qualities. She does not need to be persuaded of or converted to their values.

It is known that the perfume of any plant or flower is held in a tiny drop of volatile oil and that by distillation this oil rises with the steam that in turn is condensed into a receiver or globe fixed above the boiler. But the fragrant oil may also be secured in a way that requires no distilling apparatus, and its capture may form one of many interesting recreations open to a country housewife who owns a garden of sweet scents.

The following method was advocated in the *Journal of Chemistry* many years ago, but still stands good :

" Gather the flowers with as little stalk as possible

165

and put them into a jar three-parts full of Olive oil.
After these have soaked for twenty-four hours turn
all through a coarse muslin bag and squeeze out the
oil ; add fresh flowers to the oil, and repeat the process many times, according to the strength of perfume desired. When the odour of one flower only
is desired a great quantity of petals are needed, but
a perfume of mixed flowers will allow of using any
sweet-scented ones that come to hand . . . the
kinds to be preferred for the purpose are Sweet Pea,
Mignonette, Stocks, Clove Carnations, Pinks and
Roses.

" The oil, when thoroughly impregnated is mixed
with an equal quantity of deodorised alcohol and
shaken up every day for a fortnight (being kept in a
well-stoppered bottle meanwhile). After this the
spirit may be poured off clear and bright and will be
found to be highly charged with the scent gathered
by the oil."

It will probably be less trouble to buy scent than to
make for one's self in this way, but still the product is
worth all it has cost.

Pot Pourri

There is another way of preserving the scent of sweet
flowers that everyone loves to try who has a garden of
bloom to pick from, and that is to make a bowl of Pot
Pourri. This is one of the most delicious scents one
can have in a room, never overpowering, but gently
increased when the air of the room grows warmer.

Here is a recipe that is said to retain its fragrance for
fifty years :

Gather late in the day, and when perfectly dry a

peck of rose-petals ; put them in a bowl and strew over them ¾ lb. of common salt. Let them remain three or four days and if more petals are added put in a little more salt. Mix together a ¼ lb of bay salt, powdered cloves, allspice and brown sugar, also a ¼ lb of gun benzoin and powdered orris-root. Add a gill of brandy and a few dry sprigs of lavender and scented verbena. The mixture should occasionally be stirred but kept in covered jars, the covers only to be removed when the scent is wanted in the room. If after a time the mixture dries, add a little more brandy.

A simpler way which some would find it easier to follow would be to pick all the petals available and perfumed sprigs as well, mixing Rosemary and Lavender with Bay-leaves, flowers of Heliotrope and Mignonette, Rose-petals and Musk, drying these a little in the sun, with also some dried Marjoram and Lemon Balm and Orange-flowers if there are any. Put all into a china jar. Put in the peel of a sweet orange stuck with Cloves, a few bits of stick Cinnamon, sprinkle salt over and moisten from the top with a little brandy. Mix well together and keep closely covered when not wanted in use. If care is taken the mixture will keep for years.

The Common Camomile

Mention has been made of Pyrethrum powder for keeping rooms free from flies, but this is a similar thing to the common Camomile, the plant that is found growing wild in most parts of the British Isles. The flower is much used in medicine, in fact, an old writer calls it the Plant Physician, for not only will its flowers, when infused and drunk as tea, cure many ills of stomach and head, and its leaves dried and powdered, keep away flies and other insects, but a plant of it should be in every greenhouse, for if a sickly shrub or flower be brought near to it that will soon recover health. The Pyrethrum is a variety of the Camomile.

FIR CONES

Where fir trees grow there will be a scattering of Cones at certain seasons, and these have several uses for a country housewife. For one thing, she knows their worth as an addition to her box of Logs for the fire ; a few cones judiciously put in among dead embers will soon revive a fire. They burn with a slightly acrid odour that is refreshing and far from unpleasant, and if mingled with peat brighten up that considerably.

Many ornamental uses are devised for the smaller cones ; picture frames and boxes have been made with them, but for all such purposes they need coating with varnish as they can be real dust-collectors.

One ingenious use for very large cones that are fully opened is to make pincushions of them by inserting tiny cushions of bright-coloured silk filled with wadding between each open point. To encourage the cone to open out it is warmed by the fire, and then the spaces provided are ample for inserting a little pad, the bottom of which can have a dab of gum to keep it in place.

Cones and twigs and dried moss are all worth saving for winter fires, and may make a considerable difference to the bill for fuel if a sack is taken for collecting them.

BEECH AND OAK LEAVES : TO KEEP FRESH

The lovely colours of these leaves in the autumn make people anxious to preserve them for the winter decoration of rooms, and they gather boughs only to find they wither in course of time. Their life can be indefinitely preserved, however, by standing the branches in a deep jar holding a mixture of glycerine and water—about 8 ozs of glycerine to 2 qts. of water. Leave the branches to take up all they will, and when they seem to need no more the leaves can be placed where desired and they will neither fade nor shrivel. The glycerine preserves, too, the glossy appearance.

LEAF-MOULD

Oak and beech leaves with which the ground will be found plentifully bestrewed, should never be ignored by those who live in the country, as if made into a mound and allowed to rot naturally they provide one of the richest of plant manures. It is worth while taking a sack to collect them if one is able to spare the time to do so.

GIANT THISTLES AND BULRUSHES

These, when gathered, should hang heads downward until all the sap seems to have run from the stalks which then become brittle ; after that there will be no shrivelling.

PACKING FLOWERS AND LEAVES FOR THE POST

A word in this connection may fitly conclude this section—it is often badly needed.

Choose long, narrow boxes by preference, long enough to allow of a good length of stem being cut as this is one secret of keeping flowers fresh.

Line the boxes with waxed or thick white paper, not tissue paper. Do not pack flowers when wet and avoid sprinkling them with water.

Cut them in the bud, or when barely half-opened, never on any account full-blown.

Pack somewhat tightly, or at any rate so that they cannot shake about ; do not be afraid of their crushing each other. It is a great mistake to give flowers " plenty of room " when they are going to travel. Tulips and Narcissi and Roses should be packed alternate ways, that is, with flowers at each end of the box ; put in a very little of their own green and plenty of stiff paper. Cover and tie down securely.

Small flowers like primroses and violets should be tied in close bunches and then packed together ; ivy leaves and other leaves also are sent this way, so are small berries.

Dried Rose-Petals

It is good to know these can be put to excellent use, for a Rose Garden provides falling petals by the sackful almost every day in the season. Someone long ago suggested these should be used at weddings in place of the confetti that so many find detestable, and this is an idea well worth improving upon.

The petals should be gathered just when the rose is beginning to drop, and collected into a basket. They should be spread out on sheets of paper in a warm greenhouse or sunny garret and turned over frequently until they feel fairly dry. After this collect and fill bags—of pink muslin if you can, if not, of fancy tissue—and tie up with sarcenet ribbon.

It is an improvement to scent the petals with a pinch of powdered cloves or musk before tying up the bags.

A few hints about the Arrangement of Country Flowers and the Care of Plants Indoors may not be superfluous here.

ARRANGING FLOWERS

Sprays of Almond Blossom and of Willow (or Palm) come at the right time of the year for combining with yellow narcissi and early tulips, and the stems of the one should be cut as long as possible so as to overreach the shorter stems of the bulbs. Yellow and pink always give an effect of spring freshness, and if there are no long-stemmed holders use clips of galvanised wire to set in a dish or bowl and let that hold some moss or a clump of saxifrage.

Primroses and violets are difficult to arrange for the table but if they can be taken in a clump with a little earth and made into a mound with moss in a shallow dish they will look better and keep fresh a long time. Otherwise they look well in shallow baskets of moss.

It is a good plan when arranging flowers to have in mind the way they grow in their natural manner and keep as much as possible to the same arrangement, that is, let the tall-growing be cut with long stems and set in long flower-holders, the short in bowls or baskets, the dwarf in shallow dishes. In arranging wild flowers this is especially to be remembered, long grasses being cut long and the short blooms kept low.

CARE OF INDOOR PLANTS

Growing plants in rooms and greenhouses want an occasional " extra feed " of liquid manure to encourage and stimulate them, and this is best given by putting a little fowl or horse-manure at the bottom of a watering can and keeping this with water over it, using that instead of rain-water while the plants are flowering.

All room plants want a gentle shower-bath once a fortnight when it is possible to give it to them with a fine rose and tepid water. And they should stand in a deep tin with water half-way up the pot for some hours at least once a week. This is far better than watering them from the top at any time, and it is a great deal better than allowing water to remain in a bowl in which a pot is standing. A long drink, but not time to get water-logged, is the best treatment.

Bulbs planted in bowls require very little water until the green begins to show, and then they need to be kept moist until their season is over and they go dry again.

HOBBIES OF THE COUNTRY HOUSEWIFE, AND SOME HOUSEHOLD PESTS, ALSO FRIENDS

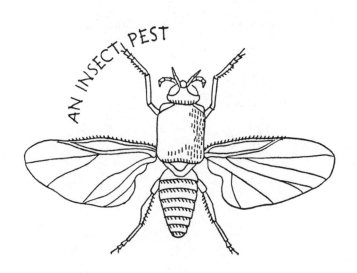

AN INSECT PEST

VII

1. *Hobbies of the Country Housewife*

MOST country-loving folk will say with the late Poet Laureate, Robert Bridges

" I love all beauteous things ;
I seek and adore them . . ."

and beauteous things for them will include Furred and Feathered pets and probably Bees. Regarding the last-named, if anxious to make them profitable as producers of honey, study should be made of books on the subject, or at least of Government leaflets that give advice in brief and can be had for a trifling sum. Bees, as those who have read their Maeterlinck know well are a race and a community about which it is not well to generalise, and about which it is hardly possible to know too much, and the housewife who is anxious to keep one or more hives will do well to study what the books say and get local advice from those who are already accustomed to keeping bees. It is quite certain that a hive is a great help where fruit is grown in quantity and especially where tomatoes are cultivated, and both greenhouse and garden will be more productive with the bees' help, but only where they are studied with care and induced to settle contentedly. When they do this bees can be of the greatest assistance to growers of fruit and flowers.

With regard to Furred and Feathered Folk, however

it is possible for us to include some general hints that cannot fail to be useful even if they are not all-sufficient and our book would hardly be complete without them.

RABBITS

In the summer-time these cost very little to feed and are useful for eating up surplus vegetable produce, in winter, when grass and clover, lettuce and other greens are scarce, their food has to be supplemented with roots—swedes, carrots and mangels, and with oats and a little " mash ". They need a plentiful supply of sweet hay at all times. Rabbits are usually fed twice daily, but young ones need food according to appetite. They will thrive in outdoor hutches providing these are proof against damp and draught and are placed against a sheltering wall. Ordinary rabbit skins are of little value unless of prime quality and free from moult. All that is necessary after they have been removed from a carcass is to dry them thoroughly in the air. They can be disposed of to fur retailers at better prices than to dealers in skins, but it is of little use to sell single skins and small quantities.

As few people care about eating the meat of rabbits they have kept themselves, it is wiser to keep breeds that yield some profit from their wool, like the Angoras, and then interest in them is doubled and made worth while. This wool is so extensively used as to be really well worth while producing, even when a good price has to be paid for the rabbit to begin with. It is used extensively for the manufacture of children's clothing and trimmings and to some extent for sports clothes, and is never cheap to buy in small quantities for knitting purposes. The country housewife who keeps Angoras for clipping is well advised to learn the art of spinning as well, so that she may make many things from her own production that she might otherwise have to buy. Angora wool garments are said to be particularly good for bronchial and rheumatic people to wear. As a rule the wool grown from British Angora rabbits is longer in fibre and of finer texture than that from French breeds and realises appreciably better prices in the wool market.

Food should be given twice daily, but three times a day to breeding rabbits and growing young, mixed green food helped with a little " mash ". " Woollers " will consume about two pounds of green food per day. Hay in short bits and any type of " seedy " fodder should not be allowed in the hutches because of its liability to get worked into the wool. A first clipping is made when a " wooller " is eight weeks old, and thereafter a clipping once a quarter. In that time the wool grows about three inches in length. A rabbit should be carefully combed before it is clipped, doing this with a brush the bristles of which are set in a pneumatic cushion ; cutting is done with barbers' scissors. About $\frac{1}{2}$ lb. weight per head is the yield from Angoras *per annum*. An average price per lb. for Angora wool is 2 5s.

DRESSING RABBIT SKINS

This is not a particularly easy task for anyone unaccustomed to the work, but it is quite possible to acquire the way of doing it and of treating the skins of rabbits bred at home that are of particularly good quality. A mixture of *Common Salt, Powdered Alum* and *Water*, 1 lb. of each to a quart, is used for soaking the skins. Soak three days, then dry by pinning up at the corners. When dry cover the inside skin with a paste of flour and water, leave this to dry then rub off and again rub the skin with pumice powder, rubbing hard and softening the skin with the hands until it is perfectly flexible. After this it can be cut with a knife on the underside and used in any way desired.

Rabbit skins make good mats for the floor, footmuffs, warm gloves, rugs and coverlets and can be pieced together and sewn on the underside with suitable thread and a furrier's needle. It is sometimes possible to get a lesson in the art of making up skins through a Women's Institute.

Using Fowl Feathers

These sometimes present a problem now that feather beds are so little used and feathers accumulate very quickly. They must await some convenient time for their sorting as not much can be done while plucking is going forward in the game season. Sorting into sizes, separating those that have quills, and keeping the down by itself, is the first operation that has to be considered. For temporary keeping the feathers were probably stuffed into a big sack.

When starting to sort feathers clear the room or shed of everything that cannot be closely covered over, and then spread an old sheet over the floor, tacking it firmly. Spread coverings over everything else in such a way that these can be gathered up afterwards and shaken so that all they hold can be collected together. Wear a close-fitting cotton overall and a dust-cap. Use a stool to sit on and a sharp pair of scissors wherewith to snip off hard ribs and ends. Pure down, such as is obtained from geese and some fowl, should have been saved at the time of plucking, so that there will not be much of this, but small feathers should be kept apart from larger ones as they are best for pillows and will need to be dried before they are used. Larger ones, still without quills and with hard ribs cut away, will fill bolsters and sofa cushions or humpties for the floor. The quilled feathers make admirable dusting brooms if carefully separated and sorted into sizes, and tied round a centre stave of wood. Long tail feathers that are not good enough for hat trimmings make feather brooms for sweeping ceilings and cornices. Thus feathers have many uses.

Game and pigeon feathers should not be mixed with ordinary fowl feathers as they are apt to have a strong scent, and even the best fowl feathers need careful picking over to ensure their being free from any taint. It is a good plan to save all the paper bags that come into the house and use these for holders, filling them with feathers as nearly as possible all of a kind. These bags can be loosely tied and left in a warm oven with the door ajar, so their contents will get thoroughly dried.

Many people prefer to *wash* feathers taken from poultry before making any use of them and it is a good plan where they are very mixed as to kind. Prepare a great bowl or tub of soapy lather, adding a spoonful of liquid ammonia to it. Use it as hot as possible. Stir the feathers well about, then lift them out by handfuls, squeezing them ; rinse in another tub of clear, hot, water ; spread out on an old sheet to dry in the sun or when somewhat dried fill paper bags loosely and dry in the oven.

Where feathers accumulate readily it is a good plan to renew pillows with fresh ones every four or five years.

Another way to dry feathers is to spread them in the sun where there is no draught of air. If not ready to put them to any specific use after sorting, store them in old cotton pillow-cases and sew these securely. If intending to make them into cushions at once, it would be well first to prepare the foundation shape and have it made up in percale or some cotton material and get this filled and sewn up securely without loss of time, as then the shape can be kept until the fancy cover is ready for it. Down cushions are the most difficult to make as the inner lining must itself be very soft and pliant, and it easily pulls out of line. Nevertheless, beautiful things are made by housewives who use up everything that comes to them, making coverlets and quilts from their own stores. Bearing in mind how vast a quantity of down and feathers is required to supply the demands of upholsterers and bedding manufacturers, and what exquisite creations are made, the country housewife need regard nothing in the nature of skins and feathers as useless. It may take time to find the right way of disposing of them, but there are collectors and traders who are only too glad to obtain them. Her own requirements should come first, but if unable to make use of gatherings and accumulations herself, let her inquire about trade requirements and see if her surplus cannot bring her a little profit.

2. *Insect Pests and Small Enemies*

A S most country housewives know, the best way to deal with flies and other troublesome pests, is to forestall their coming, for once they have obtained an entrance they are very difficult to dislodge. But prevention is by no means easy.

With Moths, for example, it is the young that cause trouble, from eggs that hatch out ; it is not the adult Moth. If the eggs are not discovered in time, as the young are hatched, they begin to feed upon the material about them and the mischief is done. The parent Moth prefers to deposit its eggs on some woolly or furry substance, and this kind of material should always be watched ; hard or smooth substances need not be suspected. As soon as the eggs hatch out they form caterpillars which are avaricious for food.

The adult Moth seeks dark places as well as soft substances on which to deposit eggs, so that wardrobes and trunks and cupboards where light does not penetrate should be watched. Open shelves and airy closets hardly need to be investigated. Garments that are kept in wardrobes should every now and then be brought into the open air and sunshine and be given a beating and shaking, letting the wind blow through them. Heavy garments such as fur coats and rugs ought to have a thorough brushing, doing this on a table in the open air. It is not a bad plan to lay them on the floor and use a vacuum cleaner over them, especially when it may not be possible to take them out of doors. Moths and the caterpillar worm cannot stand the strong suction of a vacuum and will be sucked out even when they have embedded themselves quite firmly into the fabric. The next best thing to vacuum suction is spraying with disinfectant solution, and this suits well for men's garments such as are made of smooth materials.

BEETLES AND COCKROACHES are more dreaded by many people than moths or mice, and if by ill-luck they have obtained a hold on the house their extermination must be resolved upon with as little delay as possible, for they come not in companies, but in battalions. Whatever remedy be used, and plain powdered borax for sifting into crevices is as good as anything else, it must be persisted in for at least three weeks before it can be certain that they have been got rid of. The crevices between skirting-boards and floor-boards are their favourite entrances and exits. Simply putting down traps and things that are abhorrent to them is of little avail.

GNATS AND GREEN-FLY (or APHIS)

Tobacco-smoke is the easiest way of dissipating gnats when they swarm about any spot and green-fly also yields to the same when it is pungent enough. The best method is to burn common tobacco leaves in flower-pots letting the draught carry the smoke where it will. Gnats can be cleared from a neighbourhood by burning Dalmatian Insect Powder or by evaporation Camphor held over a candle flame. Fumigating with sulphur is again an excellent remedy where a room or shed can be emptied of anything that would be injured by the smoke.

An emulsion to rub on the skin to allay the irritation caused by stings from gnats and other insects is made by mixing Olive Oil, Turpentine, Eucalyptus, Ammonia and water together. Naphthalene in flakes or cubes is one of the best remedies for destroying FLEAS, and some should be kept in wardrobes and boxes and drawers. Out-buildings that sometimes become badly infested with these troublesome creatures should be liberally sprayed with creosote or paraffin, while burning sulphur in them is one of the best ways of getting rid of all kinds of pests.

WOODLICE

The accumulation of old boxes and rubbish in sheds and outhouses is the sure way of encouraging Woodlice and other pests. This should be avoided, but if lice are present they can be cleared by using Arsenate of Lead or Paris Green to smear over boards, and especially to paint *underneath* those boards placed in hot-houses to save treading on damp earth. This is a way of getting rid of slugs and snails as well.

" DADDY LONGLEGS " AND " LEATHER JACKETS "

These two troublesome pests are more harmful underground than they are above it, as they feed on roots and are destructive to grass-land ; they also eat turnips and mangolds, peas and beans, and all species of them are injurious. They lay their eggs in the summer and autumn, and the only way to get rid of them is to dig deep enough to get at these eggs and destroy them by fumigation, that is, by using a Soil Fumigant. The larvæ are about an inch in length and vary in colour from brown to ash-grey.

Woolly Aphis

The Woolly Aphis, seen in old orchards and on neglected trees can only really be overcome by attacking the pest below-ground. Where the root form of the pest is ignored it will go on appearing year after year. Injections of Carbon Bisulphide around the roots, using a plant injector for the purpose, at least six inches below the surface and about two feet away from the roots of the tree is the most effective. This should be done in the month of March, when the soil is fairly dry.

Slugs and Snails

Slugs and Snails, which seem impervious to the usual method of sprinkling lime, salt and soot around young plants, can be routed by using Bordeaux Mixture. But the best method of keeping these in check is to let poultry and ducks find in them their natural food and where they roam freely few slugs have any chance of life. Where poultry are not kept, however, another way is to sprinkle chopped lettuce leaves round young plants and in borders, this being impregnated with Arsenate of Lead. They are greedy for this food and the lead quickly destroys them.

House Flies

The common House Fly is one of the Pests most to be dreaded because it is a carrier of dirt and disease. As Flies have an unerring instinct for garbage all refuse should be burnt when possible. To sprinkle refuse and manure heaps with Borax and use the watering-can afterwards will not harm the manure's later usefulness and will effectually prevent flies from settling.

In the house itself, two good ways of keeping it free from Flies is (1) to mix saucerfuls of milk and water with some Formaldehyde, putting a bit of bread in the middle of each, and place these in rooms overnight. A weak solution of Salicylate of Soda is even more effective. (2) Another way is to sprinkle sand and sawdust with Paraffin and spread this about in places where they congregate, and it will effectually drive them away. In houses where Vacuum Cleaners are freely used flies have little chance to settle and deposit their eggs, and the use of a good chemical sprayer is also an excellent thing as they do not like these odours.

Flies dislike the Elder tree and branches of this placed about the house are an old-fashioned but still useful means of keeping flies out of it.

Pyrethrum Powder is another very useful thing to have about and to use for rubbing into the coats of Cats and Dogs to keep them free from irritating insects. Fowls, also, should have their under feathers dusted with it and their nests should be sprinkled occasionally.

WASPS

Wasps are the chief dread of many country folk who have no fear of other things ; their time is comparatively short, however, and their presence can be warded off if care is taken to keep sweet things very closely covered. The damage they do is mostly seen in the orchard, where they are great consumers of ripe fruit ; indeed it is only possible to keep prime plums and other choice fruit from them by covering it with fine net or gauze, and this cannot always be done. Fruit under glass is easier to save because the wasps can be caught, and indeed in many orchards it is found useful to hang up long-necked bottles of honey-liquor to entice them in and so keep them from better things. The first wasp should be annihilated without mercy, as it is sure to be followed by friends.

ANTS

These come by epidemics, apparently without cause or reason and without warning. They will march in their thousands upon the house or the hut or bungalow they have chosen to invade, and will swarm up walls and over floors in the most determined manner. They are organised and are not got rid of by frightening one or two here and there. One of the best methods of dealing with them is by counter-attack, such as the digging of a deep ditch across their chosen road. In the house the one thing that affects and disturbs and eventually will banish them is Paraffin, and to spray this over floors and walls and into chinks and crevices will in a short time clear out the marauders. They will turn back on their march if they find paraffin in their path, and this is certainly one of the best things to use as it does not stain, and its odour soon disappears.

Although they are not carriers of filth and disease like flies, ants are more objectionable in other ways, and if they get into a building are exceedingly difficult to get out again.

THE MISCHIEVOUS MOUSE

Unfortunately the Mouse is more than mischievous, it is destructive as well. Where they are very persistent and are not frightened away by traps or any of the patent types of poison—which country folk cannot use if other animals are about—one of the best things to do, especially if they have got into the wood-work and behind skirtings, is to clear the house of things that would be stained, and then burn sulphur in each room for an hour or so. Powdered sulphur on a shovel, lighted with a match, will produce fumes that penetrate into all chinks and crevices. The smell is perfectly wholesome, although most unpleasant, and even intolerable, but it clears an old building better than anything else that can be devised. After the fumes have gone off windows can be opened and clean fresh air admitted, and this quickly dissipates any odour. In fact, the after-effect of such a fumigation is to create a freshness that is wholesome and acceptable. Quite a number of dead mice may be found in corners where they have tried to escape, and where holes are known to be or are visible they should have been stopped before sulphuring was begun.

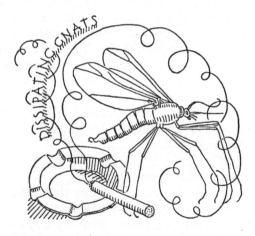

To keep on filling up crevices and to be ever vigilant is the only way to keep an old house free from visitors of this and other undesirable types. In newer buildings they can be more easily exterminated, but in old ones they have made their underground entrances and exits before their appearance in the open has been noticed.

3. *Unpaid Helpers of the Country Housewife*

T would be rank ingratitude if, after taking note of certain Helpers among the Insect tribe that are beneficial, and giving attention to others that must be dealt with as enemies, we omitted to make mention of a host of unpaid workers on the farm and in the garden, to whose toil the very existence of the fruits we have been considering is due. Without the service of

"Little things that run and quail,
    And die in silence and despair,

"Little things that fight and fail,
    And fall on earth, in sea and air,"

we should reap very poor returns from garden and field, orchard or hedgerow. Let us place on record, then, some of the debt we owe to EARTHWORMS, for example, which are every gardener's friend, since they do not destroy or feed upon living matter but upon dead substances and things that are decaying. Their own excrement, known as "worm-casts", although regarded as unsightly on a tennis lawn, is itself a valuable fertiliser. Their burrowings drain the soil and allow air to penetrate into it. If "worm-casts" are lightly swept into a heap and dried, they can be scattered over the lawn again in winter-time to enrich it. Rolling the lawn should be done *after* the worm-casts have been swept off, not before.

189

To all who keep Poultry and rear Game the Stoat and the Weasel are invaluable helpers, so, too, is the wily Hedgehog, and even to people who are not concerned with rearing pheasants and partridges these crafty little folk are still an unmixed blessing. The Squirrel, too, if not of much assistance, is still quite harmless as far as the farmer and fruit-grower are concerned.

The Owl should be called the Feathered Policeman, as he wages war against beetles, large insects, mice, voles, rats and sometimes bats. The Owl is greatly to be encouraged by farmers and gardeners.

Pheasants and Partridges consume many insects and much larvæ, and the seeds of weeds, although they also eat grain and berries, leaves and shoots. The Magpie, too, is the Farmer's friend, although it does take a little grain and some berries.

The reputation of the Hedge-Sparrow is a black one, yet often quite undeserved. Jerome K. Jerome once said, " We no more understand sparrow-nature than we do human nature, and the only case against them is how to prevent their increase of numbers . . . they are great insect-eaters as well as great corn-eaters. It has to be admitted that ripe corn in full stook is often wilfully damaged, and so are garden flowers, yet they are cleaners and scavengers as well as consumers of insects." Starlings, too, would be all-round friends if they were not so numerous, and the skylark is, on balance, more beneficial than injurious. Swallows, on the other hand, are entirely insectivorous and of great use to those whom they—literally—" take under their wing ", for they devour gnats and aphides and all manner of small insects, and do not prey on other food.

The list of beneficial birds is quite a long one and includes many that are often condemned for thieving ; the Cuckoo, for instance, feeds on the type of larvæ that is distasteful to other birds, also the harmful type of butterfly and the beetle, and it should be encouraged. The Corncrake is wholly beneficial, for it haunts the cornfields in search of worms, slugs, and snails, and weed-seeds, and does hardly any damage. The Kestrel's good deeds far outnumber its bad ones for it keeps down field-voles, frogs, mice and rats, shrews and snails, and confers great benefit as a field-worker. It is fortunate that the benefits conferred by the Goldfinch are being understood, and thanks to protection its type is multiplying ; besides being an insect-feeder, in the autumn it rids the land of thistle-seeds which it extracts from the prickles with wonderful dexterity. In spite of its liking for garden peas the Blackcap is almost entirely beneficial in its preference for insects and larvæ, and while the Blackbird does much damage through its fondness for " sampling " young fruit, this is often for the sake of getting at the juice. To put out a trough of drinking-water, big enough for the birds to take a bath if they wish, is the best way of preventing them from doing damage ; it will quite often keep them from touching the trees. The Robin's fondness for sampling ripe grapes is also quite likely to be due to thirst, and given water it will leave the fruit alone. Its natural food is earthworms, larvæ, insects, earwigs, spiders and moths, and if it rids its patrons of these it certainly deserves a bath and a drinking-trough in return !

The natural food of Rooks includes acorns, birds' eggs, earthworms and insects, but it cannot be denied that they love seed-corn, maize and potatoes. To keep them from attacking the sown corn soak a little in strong caustic soda solution and scatter this on the ground. The soda will do them no harm, and after tasting this corn they will leave that ground alone for a long time.

The little brown Wren is greatly to be encouraged as it feeds its young on the larvæ of the white cabbage butterfly, and that, as everyone knows, soon destroys a crop. The harm that Bullfinches do to orchards in spring can be prevented by spraying the trees with Quassia and Soft Soap.

A few birds of the hard-billed type are of great service to farmers and growers while they have their young to feed ; after this period they tend to seek their food more easily, but those that are entirely harmful could be counted on the fingers of one hand, and the character of these is not nearly as black as it is painted, while the number whose work is entirely beneficial are very numerous indeed.

It should be kept in mind that birds come in search of food and drink ; if their natural food is in scant supply they will try to supplement it, and Man, with his knowledge and faculties, should try to prevent damage before he starts to complain about it. When birds know where to look for food and water they will go there without seeking it in less straightforward guise. Finally, if anyone still has doubts about birds being fellow-workers with mankind, let him hear Phil Robinson on this point. Says he :

" Come out into the orchard after a shower and see the turf dotted with blackbirds and thrushes. Look at them, hard at work among the worms. Was there ever such conscientious work done before without

overseer ? . . . if you could only chalk the birds'
feet you would find that every inch of ground has
been gone over, not once but several times. How
desperately hard they work, these small fanatics !
Every dead leaf in the shrubbery will be turned over
in twenty-four hours ; all the borders and beds
patrolled ; and the whole ground searched for full-
fed caterpillars . . . even in the sunny fruit-time they
are doing good half the day, and later will come the
months of inclement weather . . . when all their
time will be spent in the incessant benefit of man.
Nor forget those months when the little tithe-
gatherers make your world beautiful with song and
" for their quiet nests and plenteous food pay with
their gentle voice ! "

BENEFICIAL INSECTS
    While waging war on Pests that are troublesome and
even injurious, a countrywoman cannot be unmindful
of others that are her friendly helpers and wholly
beneficial to have about—unfortunately, their number
is all too few !

    BEES, as everyone knows, are the most industrious
of fertilisers and blossom and fruit depend very largely
upon their activity. No bee should ever be destroyed,
not even the " leaf-cutter " that sometimes disfigures
the leaves of the rose trees by cutting semi-circular
pieces out of them for building its nests. It does no
real injury to the rose.

    LADY-BIRDS, as everyone should know, ought to
be carefully protected. These feed on Aphides
and Scale Insects, and do great service by keeping a
check on these pests. The eggs of the Lady-bird are

laid in batches on the undersides of leaves and are a pale yellow in colour. When seen they should be carefully shielded from harm.

SPIDERS and CENTIPEDES, much as they may be disliked, are also entirely beneficial, for they destroy a great number of small insects hardly visible to man.

The HORNET, the largest of British Wasps, is the only one that never does any damage to fruit, and on the other hand it consumes an enormous number of other insects. It nests in hollow tree-trunks, and is to be encouraged rather than feared.

HOVER FLIES destroy immense numbers of Aphides and feed on Rose trees attacked by Aphis. They may be recognised by a curious habit they have of hovering in the air sometimes, themselves remaining motionless, but with rapidly-vibrating wings.

DRAGON-FLIES, too, are entirely insectivorous although they do not always destroy only injurious ones. They have no sting, although country people often call them Horse-Stingers. They are themselves quite harmless.

GROUND BEETLES do much good by destroying soft-bodied insects and grubs found in the soil ; their larvæ is known to gardeners as the Slug-Killer. The harm that they do to Strawberries in the fruit season is far outweighed by their general usefulness.

The COCK-TAIL BEETLE, too, is often seen running about in gardens and should never be killed. It is a narrow black beetle about an inch long, with a habit of raising its head and tail in anger if disturbed. It feeds on slugs and insect larvæ in the soil and is an industrious worker.

Unpaid Helpers

One could wish the list of Benefactors was a much longer one, but modern methods of cultivation have interfered with the balance of Nature to such an extent that " Pests " have multiplied in unnatural abundance and where their natural food has been removed they have turned their attention to the supply afforded by cultivated plants.

Country life makes many claims on the industry and the attention of those who live it ; hardly a day may pass but what has its trials.   It makes its own peculiar demands on those who would find out its resources, and it provides work for every hour for the industrious ; yet it also gives them compensations and rewards without stint.   However busy a country housewife may be there will be few things that will not give her joy in the making, or that will not give her satisfaction when she has made them.   She is dealing with the real and the genuine things of life, and is herself a creator and not a copyist.

SPECIAL COUNTRY-HOUSE RECIPES

VIII

1. *Special Country-house Recipes*

OUSEHOLD BREAD :
½ stone country flour (7 lbs.) ;
2 ozs. dried yeast (or a gill of Brewers'
yeast) ;
½ oz. salt ;
Use milk and water in equal proportions for making into dough.

Method : Put flour into a warmed earthenware crock
or large bowl and make a deep hollow in the middle ;
sprinkle salt round this. Mix the dried yeast with
sufficient warm water to make a cream of it, adding a
teaspoonful of soft sugar or syrup. Make a " sponge "
in the hollow by working a little flour into the yeast
until it is like thick batter. Leave to ferment about
fifteen minutes. Warm the rest of a pint of milk and
water to make it like new milk and when the sponge
has risen begin to mix the flour into a dough, making
it just soft enough to handle. Use a little more
flour every now and then to clear the hands, but continue kneading until the dough looks smooth and
begins to respond by giving off a slight whistling
sound. Knead from the outer edge towards the middle
and finally make into a compact ball, sprinkle with
flour, cover with a cloth, and set in warm place to rise.
Leave from two to three hours, when it should have
doubled in quantity ; knead again on a floured board,
cut off portions for small loaves, or divide into four

for larger ones, set on baking sheets or in bread tins, allow to rise for another half-hour while the oven is getting hot, then bake for about three-quarters of an hour in good heat, but taking care not to brown too quickly.

Do not let newly-baked bread stand in a draught.

MILK BREAD

Use skimmed milk or buttermilk for mixing dough, and stir into this a spoonful of lard or melted butter.

WHOLEMEAL BREAD

Use wholemeal flour and add two spoonfuls of treacle to the milk and water used for mixing, and make dough a little softer than for white bread.

LUNCHEON CAKE FROM BREAD DOUGH

Make the sponge as for ordinary bread, using a little more yeast to half the quantity of flour. When sponge has risen sprinkle some washed currants, chopped raisins, spice and sugar round the edge and work these in by kneading. Shape into a round cake or halve the dough and put into two tins ; allow to rise until it has doubled in amount. Bake after brushing over with milk for at least an hour in moderate oven.

TEA-CAKES FROM DOUGH

Use some melted lard or butter with warm milk for mixing, and flavour with spice and sugar.

NORFOLK DUMPLINGS

When bread dough has risen and is ready for the oven it is usual to break off a small portion, make this into balls the size of a tiny orange, and to drop these into a pan of fast-boiling water. They are boiled for twenty minutes, hence are often called 20-minute dumplings. Send to table in a hot dish under a cloth. They are torn apart with two forks and are eaten with gravy or with treacle and butter, just as preferred.

BARM CAKE

3 lbs. of flour, ¾ lb. of butter or lard, 1 lb. washed currants or stoned raisins, ¼ lb. shred candied peel, ½ lb. of soft brown sugar, 1 nutmeg, grated, a pinch of mixed spice ; ½ oz. of salt, 3 eggs and sufficient milk to mix to a soft dough. Fresh brewers' barm is the best for raising, but if not to be had, dried yeast crumbled and made into a cream with warm milk will do.

Rub the butter or lard into the flour first, adding the salt at same time to ensure thorough blending. Make a well in the centre and after creaming the yeast or adding a little milk to the barm, mix a sponge with a little of the flour. Leave to rise for twenty minutes. Sprinkle the fruit, sugar and spice round the edge, beat eggs and some milk together, then start to mix the cake and to knead it like bread, adding more milk as required. Knead until an even smoothness is obtained. Allow to rise for a couple of hours in warm place, then shape into loaves, place in tins, prove another half-hour, and bake in hot oven from three-quarters to one hour. Cool, and keep ten days before using in covered tins.

LARDY CAKE

Use fresh pork fat shred or cut very finely for mixing with the flour, in the proportion of half-pound to pound of the latter, a teaspoonful of salt, and a beaten egg and sufficient warm water to mix to rather stiff dough. Knead to a ball, flatten out with the hands to an inch in thickness, set on flat tin and bake (protecting with paper) until a crisp brown crust is obtained. This cake is split, buttered, and eaten hot.

Devonshire Apple Cake

Make a rich short paste with fresh pork fat or butter, using half to a pound of flour ; mix as above with egg and warm milk. Divide into two portions and roll to even size and thickness. Cover bottom round with sliced apples and sprinkle with brown sugar ; lay on top round, press edges together and brush over with milk or melted butter, protect with paper and bake in good oven until crisp and brown. Cut into portions and eat hot with fresh cream.

Milk Batter Cakes

Make a thick batter of flour, milk, yeast and salt overnight and leave to rise in warm place ; in the morning shape the soft dough as lightly as possible using the hands, make round flat cakes and bake them in the oven after brushing over with milk. These are served hot for breakfast.

Raised Pie-crust

While used for making Pork and other Meat Pies, this is also used with Gooseberries and Apple fillings in certain country districts, and the result is excellent. Lard and water, boiled together with a little salt, are mixed with warmed flour in a bowl and lightly kneaded, then shaped with the hands round a mould, a small portion being reserved for top crust. Small green gooseberries with plenty of sugar make one filling ;

while sliced apples with sugar and cinnamon make another ; tart cherries with white sugar are also very good. When the crust is put on the pie is brushed over with egg and milk and baked to a rich brown. Eaten while fresh, with cream, these pies are delightful.

Hot Mutton Pies

These again are country specialities. In some districts they are nicer than in others. A good mode of making them is to take some mutton from the loin or breast, cut it small, season with salt, pepper, and a little diced onion, chopped mushrooms if available, and some good gravy. Make short pastry, roll rather thin and line the tins ; fill with meat, cover and brush over with milk and egg and bake in hot oven ; serve whilst still warm. There should be a good proportion of fat with lean of meat.

Pig's Fry

This is composed of the heart, liver, lights and sweetbread, and is always used whilst fresh. Wash well in salted water and simmer for half an hour, then dry and cut into thin slices ; dredge with flour mixed with seasoning and powdered sage ; fry to a nice brown and fry at same time a few bits of bacon and some chopped onion. Make a thick gravy with stock from pork bones flavoured with onion, herbs and tomato. Pour this into the middle of a shallow dish and arrange the fry neatly round it. Or the fry is served dry with apple sauce.

To Pickle Pork

A good brine for pickling pieces of fresh pork can be used again and again if it is boiled up now and then.

It is made with common salt or bay salt, a pinch of saltpetre, sugar and some black peppers, boiled together a few minutes, then strained into a barrel or pippin. Pork is usually cut into strips before it is pickled. Chaps and Hands, like hams, are cured by drysalting.

Sucking Pig

This is stuffed with potatoes mashed with milk and flavoured with onion and sage, and then is trussed like a hare and roasted, protected with buttered paper and basted often. It needs great care in roasting and is not done in less than two hours.

Hunter's Beef

Take as lean a piece as can be procured of the thin flank of beef, remove any bones and lay in a deep dish, rubbing and turning it frequently every day for a fortnight. The pickle mixture with which it is rubbed is made with rough salt, 1 lb., saltpetre, $\frac{1}{2}$ oz., moist sugar, $\frac{1}{2}$ lb., allspice, black pepper and cloves, $\frac{1}{2}$ oz. each. At the end of the time wash it and roll up tightly, secure with tape and let it simmer with sufficient water to cover it for some five or six hours. Put under light weight when taking from the pan, but do not loosen the tapes until quite cold. This is excellent when cut in thin slices.

To Make Sausages

Sausages are usually made from fresh pork, but are also made from minced beef and mutton, and are nicest when a little fat is used with the lean meat. In the country they are often made at home. The skins want cleansing with scrupulous care, and the meat should be minced and well seasoned. Use a funnel to assist the filling of the skins, and press the meat firmly down. Tie with thread. Small sausages are nicer than large. Do not keep sausages long after they have been made, but if they are not for immediate use they can be boiled for ten minutes or so and then set away and will be none the worse for later frying.

To Make Brawn

This is usually made from the head of a pig, the brains being removed and the ears cut off. The head is split down and cleansed very carefully then rubbed with common salt and a little saltpetre and left for three or four days. It is washed, covered with water, and boiled very gently until the bones can easily be drawn out. Extract these and remove the skin of the head. Cut the meat in small pieces and place in a mould. Strain some liquor and flavour it, adding a little leaf gelatine, and when this is dissolved pour it over the meat in the mould, press down with a saucer or plate that will barely cover, and weight this. As pork is deficient in gelatinous matter it is well to cook a piece of knuckle of veal or beef with the pig's head, otherwise gelatine will be necessary.

To Cure Bacon

The secret of curing bacon successfully is to keep the salt dry, otherwise the meat will be pickled instead of cured. Change the salt often if it seems to melt. If curing more than one flitch change them about, putting bottom to top and so on. Rub daily. The time taken to cure depends on thickness of the flitch and somewhat on weather. A month is the average for a moderately thick flitch in a dry season. " Green " bacon is further dried, but never smoked.

A YORKSHIRE RECIPE FOR CURING A HAM OF 10 LBS.
WEIGHT

Place in a saucepan 1 pint each of old ale and brown stout, add ¾ lb. brown treacle, 1 lb. coarse salt, and ¾ oz. of saltpetre. Bring to the boil. Meanwhile rub the ham well with dry salt and lay it in a deep earthenware crock ; pour over it the boiling liquor. Keep in this pickle about three weeks, turning the ham every day. Drain and wipe dry, then stitch up in coarse muslin and hang in a dry place for at least six weeks before using. Rub well before cooking.

One last recipe must be added, and that is perhaps the best we can give, and it is for those who have eggs to spare and milk of the best. It is called

CRÊME BRULÉE, or BURNT CREAM

To a pint and a half of rich unskimmed milk allow six new-laid eggs, yolks and whites lightly beaten together. Heat the milk in a lined saucepan, but not nearly to boiling-point. Beat up with the eggs a pinch of salt and about three tablespoonfuls of castor sugar, add a grate of fresh lemon-rind. Pour the warmed milk over the eggs and mix thoroughly, then pour the custard into a deep dish of fireproof china or Pyrex glass, and set it in a slow oven to become firm. Take out, light the griller of a gas-cooker, or place the dish before a roasting fire after first sprinkling the surface very thickly with coarse crystallised sugar or candy sugar crystals rubbed down. Let the sugar brown quickly but not actually burn. It should make a candy crust through which one would break to reach the solid custard below. The latter can be flavoured with a little brandy or a bay-leaf, as taste prefers. This sweet is always eaten hot.

INDEX

Index

Accompaniments to Game, 147
Angora Rabbits, 176-177
Ants, 186
Aphis (Green-fly), 182
„ (Woolly), 184
Apple and Blackberry Jam, 45
„ Lemon and Ginger Marma-
lade, 56
Apples and Pears, Bottling, 36 ; to
blanch, 82 ; to dry, 81 ; to store,
76
Apricot Jam, 45
Apricots and Peaches, bottling, 35
Arrangement of Flowers, 171
Arsenate of Lead, 183, 184
Artichokes, Chinese, 92, 93
„ Globe, 92
Artificial Ice-making, 22

Bacon, to Cure, 205
Bag for Straining Fruit, 43
Barm Cake, 201
Beans, Bottling, 98 ; Canadian Won-
der, 92
„ Green, to Dry, 85
Beech and Oak Leaves, to keep
fresh, 168
Beef, Hunter's, 204
Beer, Hop and Malt, 66
Bees, 175, 193
Beetles and Cockroaches, 182, 194
Beneficial Insects, 193-195
Birds, 189-192
Blackberry Jelly, 46
Black Currant Jam, 46
Blanching, 33, 82, 97
Bottling, 18, 27-37 ; Fruit for, 28,
29, 30
„ in the Oven, 31
„ Vegetables, 96-99
Brandied Cherries, 57
„ Peaches, 57
Brawn, to make, 205
Bread Dough, Tea-cakes from, 200
„ Household, 199

Bread, Milk, 200
Brine, 20
Brocoli, 93
Bulrushes for the House, 169
Burnt Cream, 206
Butter-cooler, 21
Butter, Home-made, 122
„ Wrong Flavours in, 124
Butter-making, 123
Buttermilk for Scones, 126

Cabbage, Stuffed, 108
Cake, Devonshire Apple, 202
„ Lardy, 201
„ Milk Batter, 202
„ Tea- from Dough, 200
Camomile, the Common, 167
Canadian Wonder Beans, 92
Candying of Fruits, 58
Canning, Preservation by, 78-79
Cardoons, 95
Care of Indoor Plants, 171
Carrots, To Bottle, 98
„ Dried, 86
Celeriac, 93
Cellar, Larder and, 20
Cheese, " Double Cream ", 121
„ " Single Cream ", 122
„ Cauliflower, 108
„ Polenta, 114
„ Sponge, 114
Cheese-cakes from Curds, 125
Cherries, to Bottle, 35
Cherry Brandy, 62
„ Jam, 47
Chillies, 19
Chives, 91
Churning, 123
Chutney, to make, 102
„ Suggestions, 103-106
Clotted Cream, 119-120
Cold, Methods of Producing, 20
Condiments, 19
Cordials, Fruit, etc., 59-71
Corn Salad, 91

Index

Country-House Recipes, 199-206
Court-bouillon, 151
Cowslip Wine, 63
Cream, Clotted, 119
„ Cheeses, 121
Crême Brulée, 206
Crops, More Variety in, 89-95
Cucumber, Stewed, 111
Curd, Lemon, for Cheesecakes, 131
Curds and Whey, 125
Currant Jelly, 47
„ Wine, 63
Curried Lentils, 111

" Daddy Longlegs ", 183
Damson, Bottling, 36
„ Jam, 48
„ Wine, 64
Dandelion Wine, 64
Decorative Foliage, 90
Dessert, Brandied Fruits for, 57
Devilled Game, 142
Devonshire Apple Cake, 202
Dried Fruit Marmalade, 55
„ Rose-Petals, 170
Drying Fruits and Vegetables, 80-86
Dough, Luncheon Cake from, 200
„ Tea-cakes from Bread, 200

Earthworms, 189
Eggs, Brown Pickled, 130
„ Emulsion, 131
„ French, 110
„ Nogg, 131
„ Scrambled with Tomatoes, 114
„ To Preserve, 129, 130
„ Wine, 132
Elderberry Ketchup, 106
„ Wine, 65
Emulsion to Allay Stings, 183
Evaporation, Preservation by, 80-86
Evaporators, 80

Feathered Policeman, The, 190
Feathers, Using Fowl, 178-180
Fir Cones, 168

Fish, Freshwater, 150-153
„ Packing of, 152
„ Potted, 152
Flowers and Leaves, 165 ; Arranging, 171
Flowers and Leaves, Packing for Post, 169-170
Fly, The Common House, 184
Foliage, Decorative, 90
Forcemeat Balls, 139
Formaldehyde, 185
Four-Fruit Jam, 40
Fowl Feathers, Using, 178-179
Fowler Lee Bottling Outfit, 18
Freezers, Ice-making, 22
French Eggs, 110
Fresh Leaves for the House, 160
Freshwater Fish, 150-153
Frosted Currants, 58
Fruit, Bottling, 28-37
„ Juices, Cordials, etc., 59-61
„ Preparing for Jam-Making, 40
„ Pulp, Making of, 72-75
„ Storing, 76
„ When to pick, 27
„ Wines, Easily-made, 71
„ and Vegetable Drying, 80-86
Fuelless Cooker, The, 22-23
Furs and Feathers, 175

Game, Accessories for, 147
„ and Pigeon Feathers, 179
„ Devilled, 142
„ To Prepare for Cooking, 135-137
„ Salmi of, 139
„ Soup, 141, 149
Garden and Orchard Fruits, 27
Gherkins, Pickled, 101
Giant Thistles and Bulrushes, 169
Ginger Marmalade, 56
Globe Artichokes, 92
Glut, How to Deal with a, 119
Gnats and Green-fly, 182
Good King Henry, 94
Gooseberries, Bottling, 29
Grapefruit Marmalade, 55
Grape Wine, 65
Green Beans, 85

Index

Greengages, Bottling, 36
Greengage Jam, 48
Green Beans, Dried, 85
  ,, Gooseberry Jam, 48
  ,, Mint, 94
  ,, Peas, Dried, 85
  ,, Vegetables, 85
Grilling or Planking, 136-137
Ground Beetles, 194
Grouse Soup, 149

Ham, to Cure, 206
Hare, Jugged, 138
Hay-box, The, 22-23
Hedge-Sparrow, The, 190
Helpers, Unpaid, 189-195
Herb Plot, The, 159
Herbs, For Game, 141
  ,, Kitchen, 160-162
  ,, To Pick and Store, 161, 167
  ,, Useful and Fragrant, 152-158
Hobbies and Pets, 175-180
Hop and Malt Beer, 66
  ,, ,, Sherry Cordial, 66
House Fly, The Common, 184
Household Bread, 199-200
  ,, Pests, 181-186
Hover Flies, 194
Hunter's Beef, 204

Insects, Beneficial, 193-195
  ,, Pests, 181-186
Introductory Note, 11-13

Jam from Dried Fruits, 51
,, and Jelly, 38-39
Jelly Bag, 43
Jugged Hare, 138
Junkets, 125

Ketchup Recipes (Elderberry, Mushroom, Tomato, Walnut), 105-106
Ketchups, Some Suggestions, 105-106

Kestrel, The, 191
Kilner Jar, The, 18
Kitchen Herbs, Planting of, 160
  ,, ,, to Sift, 162

Lady-birds, 193
Larder, A General Survey of, 17
Larder and Cellar, 20
Lardy Cake, 201
Lavender, Dried, 163
  ,, Oil of, 163
Leaf-mould, 169
" Leather Jackets ", 183
Leaves, Beech and Oak, To keep, 168
  ,, Fresh for the House, 164
  ,, Uses for Flowers and, 165
Lemon Curd for Cheesecakes, 131
Lemon Jelly Marmalade, 55
Lentils, Curried, 111
Lettuce, Stewed, 112
Loganberries, Bottling, 37
Luncheon Cake from Bread Dough, 200

Macedoine of Vegetables, 107
Maize Flour Toast, 113; and cheese, 115
Making, Butter-, 123-124
Mangel-Wurzel Wine, 70
Marinade, 20
Marmalade, 53-56
  ,, Apple, Lemon and Ginger, 56
  ,, Dried Fruit, 55
  ,, Grapefruit, 55
  ,, Household, 53-54
  ,, Lemon Jelly, 55
  ,, Transparent, 54
Marrow Flowers Stuffed, 109
  ,, Jam, 49
Marrows over an Arch, 90
Mead, 67
Mercury, 94
Mice, 186-188
Milk, 11, 119-132
  ,, Batter Cakes, 202
  ,, Skimmed, 126-128
Mint, Green, 94

Index

Mint Jelly, 104
  ,, Vinegar, 104
Mixing Fruits, 39
Moths, 181
Mutton Pies, Hot, 203
Mushroom Ketchup, 105
Mushrooms, Pickled, 101

Nasturtium Seeds, Pickled, 102
Nettle Beer, 67
New Zealand Spinach, 94
Norfolk Dumplings, 200

Oil of Lavender, 163
  ,, Olive, 166
Onions, Stuffed, 110
Owl, The, 190

Packing Flowers and Leaves for Post, 169-170
  ,, Fish for Transport, 152
  ,, Fruit ,, ,, 28
Pan, The Boiling- , 41
  ,, Taking Bottles out of, 30
Paraffin Wax, 19
Parchment Paper, 19
Peach Tomato, The, 91
Peaches, Bottling, 35
Pears, Blanching, for Bottling, 33
  ,, Storing, 76
Peas, to Bottle, 98
Pectin, 38
Perch, 150-151
Picking Fruit, 27-28
Pickles, 100-102
  ,, To Seal, 102
  ,, Sweet, 100
  ,, Vegetable, 100-101
Pies, Hot Mutton, 203
Pie-crust, Raised, 202
Pie, Rabbit, 146
Pig, Sucking, 204
Pig's Fry, 203
Pigeon Pie, 146
Pike, 151-152
Planking, Grilling or, 136
Plank Method, The, 137

Plants, Care of Indoor, 171
Plums, Bottling, Green, 36
  ,, Greengage or Victoria, 36
Polenta Cheese, 114
Pork, to Pickle, 203
Potato Crust for Pies, 115
  ,, Provencal, 111
  ,, Toast, 113
Pot Pourri, 166-167
Pot-herbs to Pick and Store, 161
Potted Fish, 152
Preparing Fruit, 40
Preservation by Canning, 78-79
  ,,   ,, Drying, 80-86
Preserving Eggs, 129-130
  ,, Vegetables, 100-102
Pressure Cooker, The, 23-24
Provencal Peas, 111
  ,, Potatoes, 111
Pulp, Fruit, 72-74
  ,, Vegetable, 74
Pyrethrum Powder, 167, 185

Quantities of Ingredients for Jam, A Note of Warning, 44
Quenelles of Game, Rabbit or Hare, 142
Quince Jam, 50
  ,, Wine, 67

Rabbit Pie, 146
Rabbits, Care of, 176-177
  ,, Skins, to Dress, 177
Raised Pie-crust, 202
Rapid Boiling for Jams and Jellies, 42
Raspberries, Bottling, 34
Raspberry Jam, 50
  ,, Vinegar, 68
Recipes for Combining Vegetables, Cheese, etc., 107-116
Recipes for Jams and Jellies, 45-52
  ,, For Chutney, 103
  ,, Special Country-House, 199-206
Red Currant Jelly, 47
Rhubarb, Early, 34
  ,, Jam, 51
  ,, Wine, 69

Index

Rice Fritters Sweetened, 116
Rissotto, 114
Robin, The, 191
Rook, The, 191
Rose-Petals, Drying, 170
Rubber Rings, for Bottling, 18
Runner Beans, Dried, 85

Salad, Corn, 91
Salsify, 91
Salmi of Game Birds, 139
Sausages, To Make, 204
Savoury Herbs, 141
Scones, Buttermilk for, 126
Scrambled Eggs and Jerusalem
    Artichokes, 115
 ,, ,, ,, Tomatoes, 114
Shallots, Pickled, 101
Sherry Cobbler, 69
" Single-Cream " Cheese, 122
Skimmed Milk, Uses for, 127
Sloe Wine, 70
Slugs and Snails, 184
Small Vegetable Crops, 89
Sorrel, 90
Soup, Game, 141, 149
Spice-Cupboard, The, 19
Spiders and Centipedes, 194
Spinach Beet Cakes, 112
 ,,   ,, Fritters, 112
 ,,   ,, New Zealand, 94
 ,,   ,, Pulping, 74
 ,,   ,, Purée, 112
Sportsman's Bag, The, 135-153
Sterilise, How to, 30
Sterilising Pan, 18
Storage of Fruit, 76-79
Storeroom and Larder, 17
Straining Fruit, 43
Strawberries, Bottling, 34
Strawberry Jam, 51
 ,, Sherbet, 68
Stuffed Cabbage, 108
 ,, Onions, Peppers, Tomatoes,
   109-110
Sucking Pig, 204
Sulphuring Jars, 33
Sweet Pickles, 100
Syrup, Light and Heavy, for bottling
 purposes, 29

Tea-cakes from Bread Dough, 200
Terrine, To make a, 140
Testing the Seal of Bottles, 30
Thistles, Giant, for the House, 169
Time to Pick Fruit, 27
Toast, Maize Flour, 113
 ,, Potato, 113
Tomatoes, to Bottle, 32
 ,, Stuffed, 110
 ,, The Peach, 91
Transparent Orange Marmalade, 54
Tray, A Drying, 81
Trout, Fresh, 150
 ,, Salmon, 150

Unpaid Helpers, 189-195
Uses for Flowers and Leaves, 165

Vegetables, Drying, 85 ; bottling,
 96-99
Vegetable-Marrows, Stuffed, 110
 ,,   ,, To Train, 90
 ,,   ,, Jam, 49
Vegetable Pulp, 74
 ,, Plots, The, 89-95
 ,, Pickles, 100
 ,, Pie, 107
Venison, 142-145
 ,, Pasty, 144
 ,, Pudding, 145
Victoria Plums, 36

Walnuts, Green, To Pickle, 101
Walnut Ketchup, 105
Wasps and Ants, 185
Water-cooled Safe, The, 21
Water-glass for Egg-preserving,
 129
Watering Room Plants, 171
Water Souchy, 151
Weighing Fruit and Sugar, 41
Whey, 125
Wildfowl, 135-137
Wines, Home-made, 62-71
Woodlice, 183
Wren, The, 192

If you have enjoyed this Persephone book why not telephone or write to us for a free copy of the Persephone Catalogue and the current Persephone Quarterly? All Persephone books ordered from us cost £10 or three for £27 plus £2 postage per book.

PERSEPHONE BOOKS LTD
59 Lamb's Conduit Street
London WC1N 3NB

Telephone: 020 7242 9292
Fax: 020 7242 9272
sales@persephonebooks.co.uk
www.persephonebooks.co.uk